KU-288-505

Don't You Leave Me Here

ISLINGTON LIBRARIES

3 0120 02686558 4

Don't You Leave Me Here

MY LIFE
WILKO JOHNSON

Little, Brown

LITTLE BROWN

First published in Great Britain in 2016 by Little, Brown

1 3 5 7 9 10 8 6 4 2

Copyright © Wilko Johnson 2016

Lines from 'Tu Kitni Achchi Hai – O Ma' copyright © Anand Bakshi 1968

The moral right of the author has been asserted.

All rights reserved.
No part of this publication may be reproduced, stored in a
retrieval system, or transmitted, in any form or by any means, without
the prior permission in writing of the publisher, nor be otherwise circulated
in any form of binding or cover other than that in which it is published
and without a similar condition including this condition
being imposed on the subsequent purchaser.

A CIP catalogue record for this book
is available from the British Library.

ISBN 978-1-4087-0800-2

Typeset in Bembo by M Rules
Printed and bound in Great Britain by
Clays Ltd, St Ives plc

Papers used by Little, Brown are from well-managed forests
and other responsible sources.

MIX
Paper from
responsible sources
FSC® C104740

Little, Brown
An imprint of
Little, Brown Book Group
Carmelite House
50 Victoria Embankment
London EC4Y 0DZ

An Hachette UK Company
www.hachette.co.uk

www.littlebrown.co.uk

For Irene Knight 1948–2004

PROLOGUE

We flew into Tokyo in the pouring rain. Tokyo in August is so hot and humid the streets are like a steam room that almost knocks you off your feet when you step out of the air-conditioning. When the warm rain falls it does so vertically, copiously and relentlessly. I had come to Japan with my band to play at the big Fuji Rock festival for the very last time. The cancerous tumour that was killing me was now visibly swelling in my stomach and the doctors had reckoned my time in months.

At the festival site the rain continued to fall, making the ground succulent underfoot, beating on tents and umbrellas and thousands of people.

We played that night in a jam-packed and overflowing circus tent. The news of my terminal illness had been widely reported, and we stepped on stage to a wild and emotional ovation that continued throughout the show.

Well, you can't go wrong on such a scene. We played real good, and they called and called for more.

The next day we were to play on the big outdoor stage. The rain continued to fall. Waiting in the wings – walking in nervous circles with my guitar as the adrenaline took hold – my guitar would no longer lie flat against my stomach but pointed forward, pushed by the tumour – when I played, it would rock to and fro on the bloody thing. Just before we walked on stage the rain suddenly stopped, the clouds parted and the sun came shining down. The crowd, stretching from the stage into the distance, erupted in a tumultuous welcome for ourselves and for the sun.

Again we didn't go wrong. There is a special feeling you can get while performing – to see the crowd reacting to the music, faces smiling and arms waving as they join you in this celebration, this huge conspiracy to have a good time. It's a very human feeling. I was riding on this, my heart filled with happiness and love for these thousands of strangers, when thoughts of my impending death came into my mind. The feeling of joy grew stronger – these people would live on to remember this and have more such good times after I was gone, and I wished every one of them well.

After the show the rain began to fall again. They told me that in Japanese a person who brings good weather is known as a 'sunny man' . . .

CHAPTER 1

My name is Wilko Johnson. I was born John Wilkinson on 12 July 1947 on Canvey Island in the Thames Estuary. I had a sister three years older than me, Margaret, and then a brother, Malcolm, a year younger. Canvey Island is reclaimed marshland built by Dutch engineers in the seventeenth century; flat land surrounded by a sea wall which protects it from the high tide – I like to boast that I was born below sea level.

In my childhood the island was a place of farms and unmade roads where people lived in roughcast bungalows, wooden houses, caravans and even railway coaches. The level fields were terminated by oil tanks and the chimneys and towers of the Shell Haven oil refinery on the western horizon. My mother told me that the big tower was called a 'cat cracker' – quite a thing to tell a five-year-old boy.

This refinery looked down over my childhood and

3

growing up. At night it was a blaze of electric lights, with huge flames pouring from the stacks. When the sky was overcast the flames would reflect on the clouds above, casting a flickering Miltonic light over the island as if it were a remote suburb of Hades. But in the daylight, in the distance, the towers could look blue and ethereal.

In February 1953, when I was five and had just started school, there was a disastrous flood on Canvey Island – very high spring tides had combined with storm winds to produce a great wave which swept round East Anglia and into the Thames Estuary, where it hit Canvey Island. In the middle of the freezing night, part of Canvey's sea wall – built three hundred years before – collapsed, and the sea poured in on caravans and bungalows and their sleeping occupants. Fifty-six people lost their lives.

Because of my father's work as an on-call gas fitter, we had that rare thing, a telephone – Canvey 113 extension 9 – which was connected to the gas-company switchboard. This telephone meant we received some kind of warning of what had happened and we prepared to escape. I remember early that morning waiting at home to be evacuated and looking out of the back kitchen window. Where there had been flat fields, stretching away to the oil depot tanks, was now the sea – grey water with real waves coming right up to our door. Our house was in the sea. I understood perfectly well what was happening, but was fascinated by this surreal sight – green fields replaced by choppy water. (In fact it ruined our house – estuary water is not just water – it's sludge, and a plasterboard and breezeblock bungalow is not waterproof.)

The island was completely evacuated – only troops and essential workers were permitted to stay. As a gas fitter, my father was needed to maintain the gas pipes, and he was one of those who remained, wading through deep freezing water to carry out his maintenance work. It destroyed his health. He suffered chronic chest complaints from then on – bronchitis, pneumonia, asthma, you name it. Everything except cancer, and it grew worse every autumn. Canvey was often enveloped in mist and fog at that time, sometimes very mysterious and beautiful, but no good for damaged lungs. He couldn't breathe. Eventually he had to give up his job as a fitter, riding round on his bike, and take a sedentary indoor job looking after the stores. Each year his lungs grew weaker when the fog came down. After ten winters it killed him, at the age of fifty-six. Although his work for the gas company had caused his death, my mother never received a full pension, because he had died a few months before achieving the required length of service. They continued to send gas bills in his name long after he died.

I hated him – he was stupid, ignorant and uneducated, and had an evil temper. And he was violent; once he was holding a saw and in a fit of temper he struck at me with it. I fell over and the teeth of the saw cut a line across my leg. This was when I was a child. I never suffered the horrific violence one sometimes reads of in the newspapers. Nothing like that – nothing to cause concern in a normal working-class neighbourhood – but I do know the terror of a child being violently assaulted by an adult – and by the very adult who is supposed to be a protector and a refuge. I've never laid a finger on my own kids.

The atmosphere in our home was poisoned by him. He had been a soldier for some years in India, on the North-West Frontier of the British Raj and then in World War II, and he had a row of medals which he would put on every Remembrance Day, when he would take us down to the war memorial for the service. I don't know what the medals were for – I like to think he did something brave. When I came home one day at the age of sixteen to find he had died, I felt elated and free.

Anyway, after being evacuated from the flooded island, we went to stay with relatives in Sheffield. When we arrived, there was a broadcast on the wireless from the reception centre where the Canvey Island refugees were gathering. A character called Wilfred Pickles, a popular radio and TV presenter, was interviewing people, and we heard him say, 'We've got little Johnny Martin here and he's going to sing a song for us.' Yes, it was my chum Johnny Martin, from around the corner. He sang 'Me And My Teddy Bear'. And so 'The Big Figure' became the first member of Dr Feelgood to make it on to the airwaves. And with a national audience too.

We stayed in Sheffield for some time. Malcolm and I even attended school there, although he was too young. We were introduced to the other kids as refugees from the Canvey Island flood, which was front-page news at that time.

We were very close as brothers, though rather different in temperament. Malcolm has always been a very serene guy – I have never seen him in a rage. He is a gifted painter and classical guitarist. I am none of these things, and serenity doesn't come easily to me, but me and Malc, we've been really good friends all our lives. We often, after sitting a long time in silence, suddenly speak the same random word together.

So there we were, listening to our pal Johnny Martin singing, rather breathlessly, on the wireless. Johnny Martin. The Big Figure.

Figure's mum and dad appeared somewhat bohemian and artistic in our working-class neighbourhood. His dad played the guitar and his mum the accordion, and his mum ran a dance class called Peggy Martin's Troupe. Figure and I always enjoyed the ridiculous – when we first went up to junior school we sat together in class. I drew a big black spider inside my desk, and once, when we were making puppets, we invented this thing called a 'snitch snatcher' – it was a strip of paper twisted into the shape of a propeller and glued on to the nose of the puppet. What the purpose of these things was I don't know, but we made many of them and remembered them into adult life. I'm sure he could make one now if you asked him.

Foolishness like this typified our friendship throughout our childhood and youth. Johnny (we nicknamed him 'The Big Figure', in honour of his ample girth, at some time during our teens and he later adopted this as his *nom de guerre* for Dr Feelgood) was my pal.

We returned to Canvey Island after the flood to find it devastated. There were big blue RAF lorries in the streets pumping hot air into the soaking bungalows in an effort to dry them out. Charitable organisations had sent some relief – utility furniture, chairs and tables – for many people had lost everything. At school at the end of the day they would

7

march us into a room full of donated toys from which we could take our pick (most kids had lost their Christmas toys and part of the charity effort took note of this). I remember there were several friction-drive delta wing aircraft there that fascinated me, but I never managed to get one. I can still see these things today – aluminium with blue markings and a wailing sound as they were pushed along the floor. I can't remember what I did get.

After getting our toy we were taken to another room where donations from abroad were stored – we would be given a packet of raisins from California, a tin of sardines from Norway, some cheese from Holland, and so on. Everybody got a 'flood carpet'. Most carpets on Canvey had been ruined by the deluge and one of these flood carpets went to every house. They were obviously second hand, having been cut and hacked about to accommodate other people's rooms or furniture. Our flood carpet nevertheless intrigued me, with its strange Arabic patterning, and for years it covered our living-room floor.

I passed the eleven-plus exam. Because there was no grammar school on the island, this meant I had to travel off Canvey to school every day (on a bus, a steam train – the 8.20 from Benfleet – and another bus, the 21 to Westcliff). Thus I was separated from my friends at junior school, who all went to 'Fred's Academy', a kind of 1960s Dotheboys Hall of a secondary modern school on Canvey, presided over by the draconian headmaster Fred Watkins.

So, wearing a blue blazer and carrying a bag full of homework, I was cut off from Canvey Island and my erstwhile friends. Johnny Martin went to Fred's Academy. At school I was surrounded by middle-class boys (the first I'd ever encountered) who would never dream of going to Canvey Island – it was like the Wild West, the bad end of town. There was an English teacher who made me stand in front of the class and pronounce words like 'bottle' or 'little' or 'Battle of Hastings' so he could demonstrate the horrors of dropped Ts and aitches. Far from humiliating this Canvey Island prole, however, his masterclasses gave me a much enjoyed opportunity to show off. They never did teach me to talk proper.

When I was twelve I got a pet rat. It was a black and white laboratory rat and very intelligent – it could swim, catch things and obey orders. You could hold a biscuit and it would sit like a dog and wait for the command before running to get it. It would fetch. I made a lead for it out of string and took it out for walks round the block. We had a long garden at home and, after checking for cats, I would take the rat to the end of the garden and tell it to sit, then walk right back into the kitchen. The rat would stay in his place until I whistled, then he would charge down the garden into the kitchen and down my shirt. I could take him over the football field and let him run free. He would come when I called him. There wasn't much affection in our family and I think I directed all of mine at this rodent.

It died in dubious circumstances and I was heartbroken. It was my first experience of the awful separation of death.

CHAPTER 2

One day at school, when I was about fifteen, we went into a different classroom for a geography lesson. At the desk where I sat there was leaning an electric guitar. I was fascinated by this thing, with its shiny strings and frets, knobs and switches, its tremolo arm and the outlandish shape of the solid body. I couldn't resist twanging on one of the strings. *Twang.* I was sold. I wanted one of these things more than anything in the world. The idea of standing there armed with an electric guitar besieged by admiring girls was ... appealing.

So, next Christmas, I got a cheap electric guitar. Johnny Martin got a drum kit. We must have made a terrible noise. I was particularly incompetent – I am left-handed and my guitar was a back-to-front left-handed thing. Its cheapness was reflected in every aspect of its construction and it was almost impossible to play. An accomplished guitarist would

10

have found difficulties playing it – the strings were about half an inch above the fretboard, and pressing them down to play a chord or note was like a medieval torture. So my progress was slow.

Then I got the chance to buy a much better instrument – a Watkins Rapier. This was an English imitation of a Fender Stratocaster. It was cheap, but it was a pretty good guitar for its time, with three pick-ups that looked like chrome tin lids, a very bendy tremolo arm, volume and tone knobs, and a pair of switches of exactly the type that could be seen on many domestic appliances. My Watkins Rapier was a conventional right-handed one and I started again, learning to play right-handed, telling myself I was an absolute beginner so I wouldn't feel so dumb. It was a real struggle to play right-handed. Holding the guitar that way round was very counter-intuitive – just picking the thing up was like trying to open a recalcitrant deckchair. All day long I would walk around feeling there was something wrong, like I was inside out. But I persevered until it came naturally to hold the instrument that way round. Now, I couldn't play any other way. (But when it comes to playing 'air violin' I always hold the bow in my left hand.)

While I was re-orienting myself in this way, I began to get the hang of music – how to play chords and riffs and so on. It was the time of The Rolling Stones – the Stones, with their anarchic image and exciting music derived from great American rhythm and blues artists like Chuck Berry and Bo Diddley, Chicago bluesmen – Muddy Waters, Howlin' Wolf – and all the artists of the Chess Records label. This was the music I wanted to play.

There were many great guitar players to be heard on American records, but my guitar hero was an English guy, Mick Green, who played with Johnny Kidd and the Pirates. I remember the first time I heard Mick Green – I was walking across the living room at home when the DJ on the radio announced, 'This is Johnny Kidd and the Pirates,' and played the new single 'I'll Never Get Over You'. I was riveted by the sound of the guitar. I still picture myself stopped mid-stride in some eternal freeze-frame listening to this magic sound – twangy notes, chopped chords and a solo of powerful simplicity.

That evening I watched Johnny Kidd and the Pirates on the TV mime show *Thank Your Lucky Stars*, and I was puzzled to see only one guitarist in the band. Where was the other one? Most bands had two guitarists, lead and rhythm. I thought the lead guitarist must have been taken sick – surely this guy with his relaxed style couldn't be the one producing those sounds. But yes he was! When I found that Mick Green combined lead and rhythm (and sounded better than both) all on one guitar, I knew what I wanted to do – I wanted to play just like him.

I hated school. I hated the constant feeling of repression, of being tyrannised by mediocrities who could never have risen to any position of authority in the real world. Gazing out of the classroom window, across the sports fields, feeling a kind of bitter envy of a lone cyclist as he pedalled along the road outside the school railings. He was free – he could go anywhere he liked, when he liked, without waiting for a bell to ring, or calling anybody 'sir'.

As soon as I could, I left school with eight or nine GCEs. I was sixteen. I got a job in a Dickensian office in Chancery Lane. It was a quantity surveyor's – they surveyed quantities. I was taught an arithmetical calculation which I had to apply repeatedly to columns of figures, checking someone else's results. There were no electronic calculators in those days – can you believe it? As well as this boring work I had to make tea for the staff. There was a telephonist who said, 'Ooh, thanks – life saver' every time I brought her a cup of tea. Every time.

I had one means of relief from this purgatory. At lunchtime I would run down the two flights of stairs into Chancery Lane, then run all the way to Denmark Street. There were dozens of music shops in the area and I would spend my lunch hour gazing at the Fender guitars in the shop windows. They were shiny and beautiful – and the price tags were huge. I really used to get a kick just looking at these things and dreaming of owning one – my wage of £3 10s a week just about covered my train fare, so a Fender guitar was way beyond my means. When the lunch hour ended, I would tear myself away from the shop windows and run all the way back to Chancery Lane and start checking figures and making tea again. 'Ooh, thanks – life saver.'

Travelling to work in the early morning was miserable. Standing among the crowds of commuters I felt crushed and utterly insignificant – it was worse than being at school. I would walk to the far end of the station and gaze across the marshland at the refinery. With its enigmatic towers, pale blue in the morning light, it looked like a distant mystical city. I called it Babylon – a place where spirits were free – and I felt my own helplessness acutely as I stared at that unattainable dream.

I realised I had made a wrong move, and went back to school to get my A levels.

School in the sixth form was much more tolerable than before – in fact it was quite a laugh. I adopted a rebel pose and went around sneering at everything. One day we went on a school trip to the Tate Gallery. There was a young art teacher and his long-haired girlfriend in charge of us, and I was goading him by sneering at the works of modern art he was asking us to appreciate. I went off walking round the gallery on my own. Suddenly I was confronted by a window on to another world – a world of bright light and colour, and the vivid imagery of a powerful dream. It was Salvador Dalí's *Metamorphosis of Narcissus*. I was gripped by excitement – I gazed and gazed into that sunlit landscape and its fantastic scenes and figures. This was a colour photograph of another place, a world of dreams. I rushed excitedly back to the teacher, all my cynicism forgotten, and told him what I had seen.

He said, 'Oh, you don't want to look at that rubbish – go and see the Mark Rothkos.' I gave the Rothkos a miss and went back to this amazing new world I had discovered.

Back at school, I signed on for an Art A level and set about learning how to paint. I wanted to make my own colour pictures of fantastic worlds.

I was also taking an English A level and this led me to a great love of literature, especially Shakespeare and poetry in general. The mighty cadences of *Paradise Lost*, the intensity of William Blake. I pondered over Wordsworth's 'Immortality Ode', sure that *I* would never lose 'the visionary gleam'. I even nurtured poetic ambitions of my own – I told my girlfriend Irene that if I reached the age of twenty-two and found that I was not a great poet, I would cut my throat.

So there I was, painting pictures, reading poetry and playing my guitar.

The day The Rolling Stones' first album was released I bunked off school with a couple of friends and went to buy it. In the record shop I found a second-hand single – 'A Shot Of Rhythm And Blues'/'I Can Tell' by Johnny Kidd and the Pirates. (In years to come, 'I Can Tell' – a Bo Diddley song – would become one of Dr Feelgood's most popular numbers, often opening the show.) We spent the afternoon playing the Stones' album, and in between plays I put on my Johnny Kidd single. By the end of the afternoon I was crazy about the Stones, rhythm and blues music and the guitar of Mick Green. I set about learning to play like him, playing Johnny Kidd records over and over, trying to catch that chopping sound. Eventually I found my style – a valiant but failed attempt to play like Mick Green, my shortcomings constituting my originality.

My brother Malcolm and I had a skiffle group. I played the harmonica and violin (which I held pressed into my stomach), Malcolm played guitar and banjo, and our friend Tony Maguire the bass – an instrument made from a tea chest, a broom handle and a piece of rope. We used to put all our instruments in the tea chest and carry it down to Canvey's small seafront, where we would set up on the street and busk. We played Leadbelly songs and old blues numbers. When the pub closed we would switch to sentimental songs like 'You Are My Sunshine', and the inebriated crowd pouring on to the street could be very generous – half-crowns and once even a ten-shilling note. We usually made enough to buy hot dogs and play on the pin tables.

One day we had been playing there and three boys came up and started asking us about this music. They were some years younger than us – aged about fourteen – but their leader didn't seem like a kid. He had a very vivid personality – a kind of eager, nervous energy – and spoke in an incisive and intelligent way. After he had gone, Malcolm and I were left talking about this striking individual who had suddenly appeared and seemed so fascinated by the music we had been playing. His name was Lee Collinson, and he went on with his two friends John Sparks and Chris Fenwick to form a jug band of their own.

I began playing with R&B bands, like the ludicrously named The Flowerpots. (They were subject to constant changes in personnel, so I suppose nobody ever felt the authority to say, 'Er, about the name ... ').

My close study of Mick Green had paid off and by now I was playing pretty well. But there was one thing I lacked – Mick Green played a Fender Telecaster.

There was a Telecaster in the display window of the music shop in Southend, but it was impossibly expensive – £107 at a time when the average working-class wage was about £15–£20 a week – so I just used to stand and stare at it through the glass. I don't think I've ever wanted something so much.

Standing next to it in the window was a beautiful red

Fender Stratocaster. With its elegant shape, contoured body, tremolo arm and variety of tones from three pick-ups, the Stratocaster was the ultimate solid-bodied electric guitar, one of the great design classics of the twentieth century, universally recognised, often copied, never equalled. Beside this streamlined luxury the Telecaster looked utilitarian, like a prototype – a simple body shape cut from a slab of wood an inch and a half thick, with no further shaping than rounded edges, a plastic scratch plate and some chrome fittings – the tailpiece and volume and tone knobs. But this guitar was the object of my desire – its very simplicity excited me. It was a mean machine. Behind the glass, though, it was a million miles away – my mum would never countenance buying anything on credit, and in those days parental permission was required for any financial dealings if you were under twenty-one.

Telecasters weren't fashionable – the famous bands of the Beatles era were using Gibson and Rickenbacker guitars, not Fenders, and my dream guitar remained unsold in the shop window for a long time. Eventually, in order to shift the thing, they dropped the price to £100 and then to £90. So keen were they to sell it that I made them an offer they couldn't refuse – I put £10 down and said I would make weekly payments of however much I could scrape together. The guitar would remain in the shop until the price was paid off.

They gave me a payment card, and every Saturday I would go to the shop and pay in whatever I had saved from pocket money, school-dinner money, any money I could find – a few pounds, shillings and pence. Then the Telecaster would be brought out from the store room and I could spend the hours till closing time playing it, caressing it, looking at it, twiddling the knobs and pretending to be Mick Green. At closing time the guitar would go back into the store room and I would go back to Canvey Island – walking to save the bus fare.

This method of payment, and my paltry instalments, naturally took a long time and I think the shop was beginning to regret the arrangement, especially since people like Eric Clapton and Jeff Beck were now using Telecasters. The guitars were in great demand and very short supply, and the shop wanted the now prestigious object back in their display window. They offered me an expensive Gibson guitar in straight exchange – they might as well have asked the Queen to exchange the Crown Jewels. However, I had still paid less than half the agreed price and there was no end in sight. Something needed to be done. My girlfriend, Irene, had a Post Office savings account, and in that account was exactly enough to pay for the Telecaster. In great secrecy (her dad would have kicked me across Canvey Island if he'd found out) she drew out the money and the Telecaster was mine. God, I loved that girl. And I've still got that guitar and the payment book. But sadly, not Irene.

Irene Knight was the most beautiful human being I ever knew. A kind-hearted, generous and radiantly friendly nature shone through her lovely face and beautiful smile. For forty years she loved me, cared for me, tolerated me and protected me. Really, for richer and poorer, for better and worse, whether I was up or down, whatever I did, she stood by me. I thought of her as the one true thing I could rely on in this universe.

We met when we were teenagers. A group of us were walking home from the youth club one evening and, as we stopped at Irene's gate, I kissed her. It shook me – my heart was pounding, my head was spinning and I knew she was the one. And from that moment we were together. She was part of me. She was my better half. Everybody loved her.

She was tough enough – she wasn't scared of anybody – but her most extraordinary attribute was her friendliness – I don't know if it was her smile or what it was, but everybody who met her felt that she was their friend, even people who had only known her on the telephone – business calls would turn into long friendly chats with people all round the world. When she was ill in bed, an old lady in the corner shop said, 'Where's Smiler?'

I can't help it if I'm uxorious – she was my Canvey Island girl and I was her Canvey lover boy.

I remember the first time I visited her home. She invited a bunch of us in for coffee – me, Figure and Malcolm. There were her mum and dad – 'Come on in, boys, sit down. Do you want a cup of coffee?' This was strange behaviour to me – the idea of welcoming anybody into *our* gloomy bungalow with my father's malign presence was out of the question. As I sat there in that room, I realised that this was a truly happy home – Irene and her mum and dad, Jim and Ivy. You could feel the affection they had for each other and this home of theirs. I never knew such places existed. A well-cared-for little home and a family who loved each

19

other and loved to be together. Not like our place, full of suspicion and caution. I had for a long time been too big for my father to dare to attack me, but there were bad feelings between us. I could never have invited Irene round for coffee while he was there.

I think I suffered worst from his bad temper and violence – our sister Margaret being a girl, and Malcolm the youngest one, the baby. Malcolm and I were very close. Sharing a bedroom through childhood, we had a whole fantasy world that we would indulge in after the bedroom light was switched out – there was a thing called the Boat Game where I was the captain of the *Queen Mary* and Malcolm the captain of the *Royal Daffodil* (a small excursion steamer we had once been on). We had adventures on our ships – pirates and the like. We also used to listen for a mysterious sound in the night called The Worge. We lived in fear of the spectre of The Wicked Window Cleaner.

One night we saw a menacing shadow on the curtains of our room. It looked like some fierce monster was standing outside and we were both pretty scared. Then Malcolm said, 'Don't worry – Dad will come along and say "Christ blimey" and kill it.'

Like many a kid brother, Malcolm followed me into things – he followed me into fishing (and caught bigger fish than I did), followed me into cycling, and followed me into rock 'n' roll. One day, he started picking out a piece of Bach on his guitar and became utterly absorbed with this. He studied music and went on to become a classical guitarist. He had found his vocation, and also found something I couldn't do. He also, unlike me, continued with his painting and became an outstanding artist, winning several prizes and being exhibited at the Royal Society of Watercolourists.

Through all this our mother kept the whole thing going. She was an intelligent and educated woman and made sure we were successful at school; she was dedicated and worked hard to keep the home. She used to scrub floors at the gas company to pay for our grammar-school uniforms. She didn't like the life she led and had a snobbish disdain for Canvey Island, where my father had brought her. She made it clear she felt she was living in circumstances beneath her rightful place. So I grew up slightly ashamed of living on Canvey Island. There was little affection in our family – I don't remember ever kissing my mother – but everyone thinks their own home is normal, so that's how we got along. And that's why I couldn't ask Irene in for coffee.

But she was my girlfriend, and I had my Telecaster.

The Big Figure meanwhile had learned to drive, and had started buying cars. He loved big powerful old saloon cars like Wolseleys and Jaguars – for a long time he owned a battered Austin Westminster, a big fifties-style car that had been luxurious in its day. This went against the fashion among boy racers for souped-up Ford Anglias with fat wheels. Figure used to look just right riding along in the Westminster. But it was dilapidated – when we were racing late to my wedding, Figure was my best man and had decorated the Westminster with a length of white ribbon in a futile attempt to make the car look respectable. We were just beginning to catch up on our time when the wind blew the ribbon, which tore the 'Flying A' hood ornament off the car and away overhead. But the powerful motor got us to the register office in time.

We enjoyed driving around at night. Figure used to drive up to our house just as the television closed down for the night, and we would set off. He used to say, 'You know, I'm convinced we're gonna see a saucer tonight.' Racing down the straight road that leads off Canvey Island was a thrill, the atmosphere charged with anticipation, but we never did see a saucer, we just went to the 24-hour filling station's coffee machine, had a cup of coffee and drove home.

I wrote a poem about our nocturnal expeditions, using my zig-zag rhyme scheme – the fourth syllable of every line rhymes with the final syllable of the next.

Get your kicks on the B1014

He comes most nights – I hear his car pull up
Outside and catch the glancing blur of lights
Through curtains – drinking Nescafé, we watch
The Epilogue, *laugh at the priest, then think*
Where to drive that night. We catalogue
The usual suggestions and arrive
At the same decision as usual.
The road lies straight, lamps stream like amber flames
Shot down the wind as we accelerate,
Our talk of girls and cars, our journey's end
The all-night filling station's Robo-Serve
Coffee machine. That's it – we talk until
We're bored and then drive back. It's a routine

Which kills night after night, yet always when
We move, cabined, through empty streets, the half-
Light seems loaded with strange drama and
We thunder down an apprehensive road.

Once, he drove us to the sea wall, where the refineries are. Figure was sometimes given to impulsive actions and, instead of stopping and parking, he kept driving up the steep sea wall. The car turned and suddenly we were at the mercy of gravity. Figure shouted, 'We're going!' as we teetered on the edge of rolling in that two-ton car down to the bottom of the wall. Some unknown movement tipped the scales and the car righted itself, and we crept back down to level ground. Stupid, ridiculous and pointless. And really danger-ous, but it seemed like a good idea at the time.

Figure was prey to superstition and we often spent time by the graveyard making gothic speculations. He told me he knew of a church that was the most haunted building in Essex. 'It's really true.'

'What do you mean it's really true?'

'Well, I read about it in the library and the book was in the non-fiction section.'

We set off to investigate this fearful place the next night. There was thick fog as we drove away from Canvey Island – the headlights only penetrating a few feet in front of us. We came to a turning – a long, straight and narrow lane that led up the hill to the haunted place. Driving up, we emerged from the top of the fog to find a clear, dark night. There in the darkness was the church, surrounded by towering elms, and we sat in the car for a while building up our courage before cautiously getting out and slowly tiptoeing towards it. Suddenly a twig snapped in the trees – we started for a second, then miraculously kept our cool, looked at each other and carried on.

We continued to boldly make our way when, out of nowhere, both at once, we were seized by panic. It was as if some supernatural alarm had gone off. We gave up all pretence of courage and fled back to the car, jumped in and locked the doors. We were actually screaming as Figure fumbled with the keys. There was no room to manoeuvre in that narrow lane but we had to escape, so the car hurtled in reverse back down the lane, back down into the fog. We were screaming all the way. Driving a car at high speed in reverse in the dark while you're being chased by a ghost is no joke, I can tell you.

So I'm playing gigs with my Telecaster and my technique is now a fair imitation of Mick Green's.

There were a couple of very good R&B bands in Southend – The Paramounts (who went on to become Procol Harum and play 'A Whiter Shade Of Pale' for ever) and The Orioles, led by Mickey Jupp, who had an extraordinarily powerful and soulful voice and wrote great songs. The band also featured Mo Witham, who remains one of the best guitarists I have ever seen. I would go to their gigs at the Cricketers Inn in Southend and stare intently at Mo and see if I could catch a fraction of the stuff he was putting down. He really was good – not just technically but in the electrifying feeling he put into his playing. He only needed to hit one note and you could tell. I could sometimes see how he played a certain phrase or riff and learn how to play it myself, but I could never make it sound like Mo.

One time I went with Irene to see Mick Green playing at a college in London with Billy J. Kramer and the Dakotas. We stood right at the front watching him produce his magical sound, and at the end of the show I jumped up on to the stage and cornered the guy. What an oaf I was! I didn't even give him a chance to get off stage but stood there telling him he was the greatest guitarist in the world, asking him why he had left Johnny Kidd and the Pirates and God knows what nonsense. I had my A-level copy of *A Winter's Tale* in my pocket and got him to sign it. Years later, when I came to know Greeny, I shamefacedly told him this story of my gaucherie. He didn't remember the incident, but I was able to show him his autograph in my *Winter's Tale*.

It was no surprise that I'd had Shakespeare in my pocket at that time. Ever since my A-level studies had turned me on to literature, I'd been reading a lot and even nurturing poetical ambitions of my own. So I played my Telecaster, read my Milton and scribbled in my notebook. I began to dream of getting a place at Cambridge to study Literature. Eventually, in 1967, I went to Newcastle University to take an English degree.

CHAPTER 3

Wow! University! Three years to read and read and do great things, and maybe write great poetry. The English Department had created a new Poetry Chair and its first occupant was Tony Harrison. I wasn't familiar with Tony's work and I went to hear him give a reading at the start of term. I was absolutely gripped by what he did. Powerful, metrical and rhymed lines delivered in a grave Yorkshire voice of extraordinary intensity. I got to know Tony – he was about thirty then, living with his wife and two children in Gosforth – and I became a kind of disciple. A formidable intellect, a first-class classical scholar, he had read more books than anybody I'd ever encountered. Also a very nice guy.

Tony taught me how to run a weekly student poetry magazine – I would publish three or four poems a week from contributions in my pigeonhole. Each poem was Xeroxed on to a separate sheet and about a hundred copies were run off, then all these pages had to be stapled together with cover sheets to make a hundred magazines. This magazine was called *Penny Make* and it sold for one penny. A penny in those days was a huge copper coin the size of a medal and there were 240 of them in a pound. After standing under the arches on a Friday lunchtime selling a few dozen magazines I would stagger into the student union weighed down by cash in my pockets that was worth less than forty modern pence.

I had taken my Telecaster to college with me and pinned up a card on the notice board in the student union: *Guitarist (ex-associate of Procol Harum) seeks band* – I figured that living in the same town as Procol Harum entitled me to say this, but it did no good – I didn't receive a single reply, so I took my guitar home at the end of the first term and put it under my bed, where it was to remain for some years. Yes, I quit playing music and just became a listener to the wide variety of sounds that were happening – everything from blues to The Beatles, Hendrix and psychedelia, and of course Bob Dylan – you name it, we'd get stoned and listen to it.

It was very heaven then to be a student – revolution and poetry and music, punctuated by the wild hallucinatory ecstasies of LSD. I tried to write poetry and developed a love of medieval literature, studying Anglo-Saxon and Old Icelandic, *Piers Plowman* and *Sir Gawain and the Green Knight*.

Irene wrote me a letter saying, 'Can I come with you to Newcastle please' ... and when I went back to Canvey for the Easter vacation we got married (in those days you had to have parental permission to marry under the age of twenty-one, but this was arranged and Irene came up to Newcastle with me). Tony Harrison let us stay at his place until we found a flat. So happy, so happy! Living in sunless backrooms and attics, reading and studying and being together. Irene could always set my heart thumping – I remember a Geordie workman exclaiming as we walked out of the house together one morning 'There she goes! Lovely as ever!' I was so proud of her.

Revolution! Revolution! When it came to politics there were two issues that aroused passionate feelings – the apartheid regime of South Africa and the Vietnam war. We demonstrated – there's a hell of a kick in marching, tens of thousands strong, through the middle of London, banners waving, chanting, unstoppable. We knew we were right and the world was going to change. But there was something freaky about surrendering to that mob ecstasy and I wonder now what we were really doing. This passion persuaded many people that society, particularly the students and the workers, was becoming politicised, and that Marxist dialectical materialism was a science which explained this, and could foretell the future.

I got involved in left-wing politics and often spoke in the debating chamber, where the working-class accent, which my grammar school had failed to cure, earned me the derision of the right-wing students (they used to call out 'Alf Garnett!' when I spoke). It also earned me the interest of the Trotskyites, who wanted to recruit me, but told me that I would have to cut my 'bourgeois' hair before I was fit to join their ranks. Among all the clamouring, bickering, tiny left-wing organisations, I couldn't find one that rose far above this level of thought – there were Anarchists who wanted an unattainable paradise, and Maoists who wanted a nuclear war – the 'People's Bomb' – so, like almost everyone else, I just went with the flow, and protested about apartheid and Vietnam and dreamed of revolution. The passion was real, and scuffling on the street with the police was a kick. It felt good to be young.

There was a strike at Ford's in Dagenham and the Trotskyites were convinced that it was political, and the workers weren't striking for terms and conditions, but for social change and revolution. I went back to Canvey Island, where many Ford workers lived, and took a look around me – nobody was interested in social change or dialectical materialism. Nobody was earnestly studying and arguing over some article in a left-wing paper. In fact, you couldn't tell there was a strike on at all. The bloke next door had arranged his holidays to coincide with the strike to avoid living on strike pay. Solidarity, Reg.

When I returned to Newcastle the Trots were holding a meeting discussing what attitude to adopt to this 'political' strike. I stood up and told them my first-hand observations of what was going on down in Essex, but they didn't want to listen. These sons and daughters of judges and respected Freemasons dismissed me as a bourgeois-haired anarchist and I left the situation.

In my third year I started drawing cartoons for the weekly college newspaper. These were caricatures of university people, staff and students. My hero cartoonist was Ralph Steadman. I could never achieve his savagery, but I was pleased to be threatened with violence and even legal action on occasions when people weren't pleased with my depictions of them. I thought this would be a good way to make a living if I could – insulting people and getting paid for it – but I never continued with it after university. The last pieces of drawing I ever did were the Dr Feelgood logo and a Christmas card of the band, way back in the early days when everything seemed like fun.

My interest in medieval literature continued to grow. In my final year I found myself taking mostly medieval stuff – along with Old and Middle English, I was the only one to study Old Icelandic (which I still occasionally like to struggle with). I got a good honours degree and realised I was never going to be a poet.

CHAPTER 4

After graduating, I took the road to Kathmandu. For reasons too complicated to explain, Irene couldn't come to
India with me, but I had vowed make the journey, so I had
to travel alone. Man, I was scared – I'd never been out of
England before. I had £60 stuffed down my Y-fronts and
set off with some friends in an old ambulance down through
Europe, across Turkey, Iran, a starkly beautiful and peaceful Afghanistan and on through the Khyber Pass to India,
where we all dispersed.

Here I am in the East:

I was in Herat chatting with some Afghanis on the street.
They said we should go somewhere for a smoke, and they
led me to a dimly lit tunnel where blokes sat on either
side in their turbans and long clothes drinking tea. They
brought out a crude stone hookah with a big pipe on top
and filled it with pure black hashish. A boy came up and

dropped a red-hot coal on top and began sucking it into life. When it was aglow he handed it to me and I took a good pull.

Now that's pure dope from Mazar-i-Sharif bubbling through that water, and you breathe out a solid blue cloud of it. Wait a moment and you're gone. Kaleidoscopes and music.

My Afghan friend was laughing in my face. 'Good chillum? No good chillum! – for Afghani wery wery good, but for tourist – no good!' All pretty exotic in the flickering oil light with these fierce-looking guys and their beards and turbans and robes. But I wasn't scared – I just knew that I would soon burst into hysterical laughter, so I made my excuses and left. I was staying in a room by the bus station and I slowly made my way there and lay down.

I woke with a start and an urgent need to vomit. I ran into the corridor towards the exit. Coming towards me was the manager of the bus station, carrying a wooden cleaning bucket. A big guy with an embroidered waistcoat and sawn-off trousers, he looked like a Turkish wrestler. Fairly terrifying. He was between me and the door and I really didn't want to puke on his floor, so I sat down. I found myself in a splendid room in some palace – richly coloured silks, tapestries, pillars and fountains all around me. And soft, soft cushions. There was a feeling of absolute luxury.

I revelled in this for a while, then wondered where I was. Panic. I realised I was trapped in a hallucination and struggled for some seconds to break free. When I did I looked up and found the manager smiling down at me: 'Mister, mister, you want toilet?'

He laughed at me the next morning and said, 'Afghanistan hashish wery wery good!'

Kandahar. Kabul. Through the Khyber Pass where my father had once defended the North-West Frontier for the British Empire. Into India, living on the streets or in cheap rooms. In the Crown Hotel in Old Delhi one night we woke to find the cream cake we had bought for Pete's birthday being dragged away by a squealing piglet. We were too stoned to pursue. We were on the fourth floor. How did a piglet get up there? The mysteries of India.

Pete Hawkins and I were travelling together after the death-trap of an ambulance had got everyone as far as Delhi, carrying with us a big slab of hashish we had bought in the customs house at Pakistan, and in the Crown Hotel we began our efforts to smuggle it home to England.

We bought one of those cloth embroidered elephants covered in little mirrors, eviscerated it, and put the dope, piece by piece, inside. This was tedious work and the elephant remained with us for a long time, staring reproachfully at us in cheap rooms and on street corners, travelling with us down through the subcontinent.

By the time we reached Bombay, the elephant was looking decidedly shabby, much of the embroidery having worn away – Pete too was looking less than 100 per cent and spent his days lying down, too weak to get out and about, so the elephant was left in my charge.

I bought some silk thread and began embroidering the flowers back on to the elephant. I used to sit cross-legged under the Gateway of India or on the platforms of the

33

Victoria Terminus like the Tailor of Gloucester stitching these patterns and flowers on this custodian of our fortunes (it was supposed to provide our fare home). I got quite adept at this needlework, having to stitch in all the little round mirrors, as well as embroidering the flowers. One day I was sitting on my sleeping bag at the VT working industriously at this task when a bunch of cops strolled across and stood looking at me. These cops were part of a squad who used to sleep quite near us on the VT platform. I was too stoned to be paranoid, so I smiled at them and carried on stitching. Eventually one of the cops said, 'You will get very good price for this!' and I said, 'Well I hope so.'

When the elephant looked presentable we packed it into a Christmas parcel, addressed it in the name of the president of the University Conservative Society, and sent it off to our friends in Newcastle. Now, they had been instructed to leave the parcel untouched for at least a couple of days, so they could deny all knowledge of it. Instead of this, they seized the parcel as soon as it arrived, and ran with it out of the back door and into the arms of the waiting customs officers.

After that, everybody relied on Howard Marks.

Mr Kardoom was a massage-man who lived and worked on Bombay's waterfront, under the Gateway of India. Every evening I would go to where he sat, surrounded by his few possessions, take off my shoes and sit down on his little carpet. After a while he would ask me for two rupees and send a boy for some ganja. He said that it was beneficial to the health to smoke ganja in the evening. 'But no charas. That makes you go mad.'

One evening when I arrived there were two or three other people there. They were talking excitedly and Mr Kardoom asked me for four rupees. 'Tonight we smoke charas; Bombay black.' While we were waiting some more people joined us. One very lively guy had a plate of food which he pointed at emphatically – 'This is Indian eat! No eggs, no mutton!'

The boy returned with two small pellets of black hashish. Mr Kardoom mixed it with ganja and filled a chillum, which he lit and passed around. When it got to me I took two big hits. By the time I passed it on, I was extremely stoned. I had just begun to take stock of my surroundings when the chillum arrived at the food man. He took a blast which made him cough, and a shower of sparks burst from the chillum. The character beside him slapped him on the shoulder and rolled over in convulsions of laughter. Soon we were all helpless, aching with mirth at the splendid display of sparks we had seen.

Eventually things quietened down and the others drifted off, until there was just me and Mr Kardoom. Beyond the shoulder of the frayed blue blazer he always wore, I could see the waves lapping to the beach in the darkness. Huge reptiles were marching in infinite solemn processions from the sea up into the streets of Bombay . . . I was in a temple staring at the wall where a thousand garish idols were expounding primeval truths with intricate mathematical gestures. They raised their arms and flowed into a massive brightly coloured mandala. In the centre sat Mr Kardoom. His eyes met mine.

'You walk in the sky?'

35

'Yes,' I said, and the word echoed and re-echoed in my skull. I stood up and took my leave and began the long walk up to the great Victoria Terminus where I slept each night. Some limousines had pulled up outside the Taj Mahal Hotel and a party of rich people was walking across the red carpet. The men were in immaculate evening dress and the women wore expensive glittering saris. I realised how scruffy I was, and that I would soon be walking among them. It was ludicrous beyond all bearing.

I stepped off the pavement and walked into the middle of the street, threw my head back and laughed out loud. The seventies were about to begin.

I met a lot of interesting people in India, including a pig. I was living on the beach in Goa. Goa was undeveloped at that time – no electricity or sanitation in the fishermen's huts among the palm trees, water from the well – primitive. I was suffering from an upset stomach and needed regular visits to the privy. These latrines consisted of a little palm-leaf hut with a concrete podium with a hole. There was also a hole on the outside – this was for the local pigs who relished faeces and would eat it all up. Quite a good sewage system. One time I was squatting there when I heard a pig trotting across. My stomach was bad, believe me, but the pig thrust his nose straight under me and began eating with great relish. I looked down at him. He had his face on the side, the better to suck up his repast. His eye was looking up at me. What else could I do? I started pissing in his eye but, apart from blinking a bit, he just carried on eating. I said to him, 'You are the filthiest bastard I have ever met.'

I also met a cop. We were standing on one of Bombay's smaller stations and I'm slightly paranoid about some drugs in my pocket. These railway cops are dressed in khaki with a colonial-style pith helmet. They also carry a big heavy stick. This guy was trying to impress me with his authority and importance. There was a small group of beggars sitting on a nearby bench – a grey-haired grandmother and three small children. The cop suddenly shouted, 'These people are not permitted here!' Then, without giving anyone a chance, he strode over and hit the grandmother on her arm with his stick. Hard. The beggars ran away. I stood looking. To my eternal shame I said nothing. I had witnessed a small atrocity: a grandmother viciously beaten in front of her grandchildren, and all to impress me. And I said nothing. I cannot recall this incident without hanging my head in shame. It makes you think – what would you do if a time ever came when we had to fight or resist oppression? *A dog's obeyed in office.*

But there are pukka gents in this world. Sitting in the dust in New Delhi one time, starving, my sole means of income a bag of Tibetan grass I had brought from Kathmandu, I was down and out and I was dirty. A smartly dressed Sikh came up to me, and asked, 'Where are you coming from?'

I said, 'England.'

He exclaimed, 'Then you are real pukka Englishman!'

It felt weird sitting there in the dust and being addressed so politely. But then he insisted that we should go to a restaurant as it was his lunch hour. He bought me a meal (a rare thing for me at that time). We chatted about England and India for a while, then he left to go back to work. I think he must have seen how hungry I was, and then made this tactful act of charity to a real pukka Englishman. He told me his name was Mr Singh.

We were on our way to Goa, standing on the gangway of a ship and talking to this American girl when she looked at Pete and said, 'Oh, you've got hepatitis.' And it was true – Pete was yellow, the whites of his eyes like yellow fish skin. This explained the terrible lethargy he had been feeling. As soon as we got down to Panjim, Pete went into the hospital there and I went down to Calangute beach.

On Christmas Eve, in this shack on the beach, I woke to the sound of classical music. It was magnificent and I dearly wished I had the knowledge or means to write it down – I listened for a while, then got up and walked out to the beach.

The sky was on fire and thronged with angels. There were choirs and choirs of them. The whole heavenly host, cherubim and seraphim spreading their wings in exaltation above the flames while the great organ-like music sang *Hallelujah*. There was one of those triangular warning signs silhouetted against the blazing sky. I knew it was Armageddon.

Back inside the shack everyone was asleep. The music faded away. It was Christmas morning. I walked back out to the beach and saw three ships come sailing in; they were those sharkfin-sailed catamaran boats that the fishermen used. Christmas Day in the morning. Something was wrong. I took a piss and it came out like Coca-Cola. I had hepatitis.

I made my way to the hospital at Panjim and arrived there just as Pete was leaving. He went to the beach. I went to the hospital where they put me in a ward with six other souls. For some reason a nurse would come in and count us every morning, so I learned to count to seven in Hindi – *ek, do, teen, chaar, panch, che, saat* . . . Nobody spoke English there, so I had to communicate in pantomime. If I needed to say anything in English to the doctors, my estuarine accent baffled them, so I had to adopt a Hindu accent. I could never get the head movements right.

Somehow or other they had got my name as 'William' and the nurse used to greet me each day with 'Good morning, William', which was rather pleasant.

The treatment for hepatitis is rest and abstention from protein, and this means that you live on powdered glucose, like icing sugar, and a little rice. This glucose is revolting on first acquaintance and makes you wonder how you can eat a whole box of it every day, which was required, but you soon get quite addicted to it, in fact you love it. But it's an austere diet and makes you crave just a little flavour. After a week or so I was allowed some curried fish with my rice – it was the second most delicious thing I had ever tasted. (The most delicious was sandwiches made with factory-made sliced bread and those little bananas they call plantains, which used to be my staple diet when I was living on the Victoria Terminus station in Bombay.)

When I first got into the hospital there was a drunken,

ragged guy who kept hassling me. I think he was showing off his English – 'I am MA! Oxford!' I was feeling
very ill and weak and unsociable and this fellow became
something of a nuisance. One night while everyone was
asleep he came along the boardwalk, drunk and singing
an extemporised ballad about living in Goa. He walked
into the ward, switched on the light and slumped on to
an empty bed. I sat up and said, 'Oi, switch that fucking
light off and shut up!' He got to his feet and began snarl-
ing angrily, then took off his shoe and threw it at me. I
jumped out of bed and went for him and he ran away out
of the door shouting, 'You are not Englishman! You are
South American!'

In the morning I was a hero and could catch the word
'light' and gestures appropriate to throwing of shoes in the
happy conversations.

But it was tedious in that ward with nobody to speak
English to and mosquitos, dogs and wildlife running free.
One evening a large dragonfly flew into the ward and was
buzzing and flapping its wings all around the room and
crashing into things. It was freaking me out. It came to
rest hanging on a cobweb high up on the wall. It wasn't
stuck, it was just resting. I wanted it to go away.

Then, out of a crack in the wall nearby, there came a
lizard. It was about two feet away from the dragonfly and
started moving across the wall. It was moving so slowly –
slower than the hands of a clock – the only way I could tell
it was moving at all was by saying, 'Now its left hand's in
front,' then minutes later, 'Now its right hand.' I watched
closely for half an hour or more as it moved towards the

dragonfly. I wanted it to kill the dragonfly so I would no longer be disturbed by its buzzing and flapping.

The lizard's nose, after a long time, was within a centimetre of its prey. Suddenly it struck, seized the huge insect and dragged it across to its crack in the wall. But it hadn't killed it and the buzzing and flapping became frenzied. The dragonfly wouldn't be pulled into the crack. My hopes of an undisturbed night were gone as they fought and buzzed and flapped in this primeval combat. Oh well, it killed a couple of hours.

As for the mosquitos, sometimes I accumulated good karma by letting them drink freely, at other times I engaged in wholesale slaughter. Canvey Island was the last place in England where malaria was endemic, so this enmity runs deep. Childhood summers on Canvey were always accompanied by mosquito bites and calamine lotion.

They discharged me from the hospital after a couple of weeks. I begged them for one final box of glucose and went back to the beach, where Pete and I were so weak that tiny waves knocked us over whenever we went into the water. I spent a while longer at that beach, recovering my strength, but I wanted to get away from there. I didn't travel all this way to get stoned on some palm beach – I wanted to be in India with Ganesh the elephant god, and Krishna and Shiva and Buddha.

I set off to travel to the fabled city of Kathmandu, leaving Pete to continue on south. Twenty hours on a boat to Bombay, forty hours on a train to Calcutta to get a Nepalese visa, then a thirty-six-hour ride to the border. I was the only European in third class and I slept with my bag tied to my wrist.

I spent my first night in Nepal in a room at the bus station where I slept deeply after my long train ride.

When I woke up I was blind. Stone blind. I jumped up in a panic and stumbled round the room. I found a tap and washed my eyes in cold water. Blurred vision returned. After a while, I could see clearly again. What had happened was this: mosquitos had bitten my upper and lower eyelids. Nowhere else. I told you it runs deep.

I found a seat on a bus and set off for Kathmandu. You travel miles over flat plains, past the birthplace of the Buddha, until suddenly the Himalayas rise as if they have been thrust from under the ground. It's startling to see these huge mountains rise up before you – and that's just the foothills.

Kathmandu was magic then – it was before the tourist trade started, it was just hippies and the occasional mountain climber who came there. I spent my time wandering round the temples and town, stoned on the legal dope. I had a room right inside the medieval city. You reached this room by an outdoor staircase. It was an attic and cost five rupees (about 10p) a day. It had a little balcony with shutters. In the morning I would open these shutters and smoke a chillum. Outside, the city would be hidden in mist, then slowly, as the sun began to rise, the shapes of the temples and pagodas would emerge from the mist, becoming more and more real until the clouds vanished and the mighty Himalayas stood looking down on this beautiful place. I used to enjoy this show every morning, then spend the day wandering alone among the stupas and shrines and temples.

In the evening there was a restaurant where all the freaks

used to go – chillums being passed around, Bob Dylan on the record player, everybody pigging out on banana fritters.

Sometimes I would go there in the daytime, and I would see this young girl running around in a cotton shirt – I supposed she belonged there. Now the nights in Kathmandu are freezing, and one night I stepped out of the restaurant, very stoned, when I felt something tugging at my sleeve. It was the girl from the restaurant. She was still wearing only a shirt and there was frost on the ground. She pointed across the street to where two more children were huddled in a doorway.

She said, 'Please give me ten paise for one milk tea.' The precision of her English was heartbreaking.

I looked down at her: I was stoned, full of food, wrapped in warm clothes, with a British passport in my pocket that could take me far from there at any time, and she was on that freezing street.

Poor naked wretches. Wheresoe'er you are,
Expose thyself to feel what wretches feel
That thou may'st shake the superflux to them.

I gave her some rupees and walked back to my room crushed by guilt. Superflux.

There was a long straight road leading down by Kathmandu and one evening I was walking back along there. The air was full of the dust of evening, and kite hawks were wheeling in the sky. I walked along past people and ox carts and looked down that evening road, and I wondered what had brought me here, so far from Canvey Island. It was like an eternal moment of destiny. I knew

I would never forget walking down that dusty road to Kathmandu. And I never have.

I wanted to get a Tibetan dragon rug. I flung my nylon sleeping bag over my shoulder and made my way to one of the Tibetan refugee settlements that surround Kathmandu. This was the accepted method of doing trade – the Tibetans, with all their hand-crafted rugs and so forth, are very keen on nylon sleeping bags. Mine was a particularly garish one, covered in big blue roses – just the job. I walked into the village and was soon called across to a doorway. I could see this bloke had some spectacular stuff in his house – yards-long banners with dragons in heavy silk, Buddhas enough to grace a temple. But first we had to drink Tibetan tea. Tibetan tea is black tea drunk cold. It is flavoured with rancid butter and salt. I drank mine with equanimity and my host was polite enough not to insist on a second cup.

He was obviously proud of all his stuff, which he must have brought across the border from Tibet when the Dalai Lama fled the Chinese. He showed me treasure after treasure, and finally a little dragon rug which he would trade for the sleeping bag. We struck our bargain and I carried my prize back to my cosy room to join the other bits and pieces I had accumulated on my travels.

When the chilly night came down I found that my dragons, however fierce and charming, could not keep out the cold like those hideous blue roses. I realised that my sleeping bag had been something of a comfort blanket for me and I missed its scruffy presence acutely.

One day on the street this Tibetan stopped me, holding a big bag full of grass.

'Ten rupees,' he said. I already had some dope and easily knocked him down to three rupees. When he had gone I wondered if the stuff was any good as he had let it go so cheap. I sat down on the street and rolled a joint. By the time I stood up I was smashed. It took me a long time to find my way through the ancient streets to my room. I carried this bag back to India with me.

Leaving Kathmandu, you stand in the dark early morning at the place where the empty trucks wait to start their journey back down to India. You can get a cheap ride on the back of one of these trucks. It was a dangerous mode of transport, frowned on by the authorities, so foreign travellers had to sit down and hide before setting off. When I was stepping off the pavement to get on to one of the trucks I slipped and twisted my ankle and fell to the ground. My heavy rucksack landed on top of me and I was in agonising pain. To hear somebody cursing and swearing in a foreign language is always amusing, and the Tibetans and Nepalis stood round me thoroughly enjoying the entertainment.

I have never been at ease with mountain scenery (perhaps it's my marshland origins, where the scenery is made of sky), but the Himalayas are magnificent beyond thought. The lap of the gods. And the Nepalis love their mountains. Every time the truck drove over some mountain pass, all the passengers would stand up and gaze in wonder at the gigantic unearthly vistas revealed.

Eventually, back in India, I limped into the holy city of Varanasi, where they burn the dead by the sacred River Ganges. I had one £5 note left and I had fallen in with a

Dutch oik called Ron who was poncing off me mercilessly. There was a post office strike on in England, there was no means of getting money, and nobody knew where I was.

We were at the burning ghats by the river when we were approached by an Indian who hassled us to go to his brother's silk shop. It was up in a loft, a place full of silk – saris, scarves, shirts, all kinds of clothes, like something out of the Arabian Nights. We sat down to tea with these guys. My ankle was still in pain and they gave me a piece of opium to eat. Apart from the pleasant effect of the narcotic, the pain in my ankle was soon completely gone.

They knew we didn't have much money and we haggled about some small items. I wondered if they would change my £5 note, but they offered a lower rate than I knew I could get in Delhi, so we left.

The next day I realised I needed some rupees and I told Ron I was going back to the silk shop to change my fiver at whatever rate. When I got there the guy greeted me and began trying to sell me a silk scarf – one of those Shiva scarves in gold with red printed patterns. It was a very good one, so I made him an offer. 'I'll give you this five-pound note, and you give me the scarf' – which didn't cost a great deal – 'and the balance in rupees.' He did some calculations and told me his offer. My heart stopped. He had made a mistake and was going to give me more in rupees than the fiver alone was worth. It was a serious miscalculation, a factor of ten. This money could get me back to Afghanistan and then home. I don't know if my voice trembled when I replied. I couldn't believe it! An Indian silk merchant making so great an error with money!

Starvation and the end of my folding money overruled any morality on my part. This was a gift from heaven.

Then they found they didn't have enough rupees in the place. I went through the agony of hearing them discussing the deal again. Surely they must notice? But no. One of them went off somewhere to get the rupees. While we were waiting, my heart was pounding and I was talking and talking about everything except money. The other guy came back and began counting out the money into my hand. Surely *now* they must realise. But no.

I was climbing down the ladder holding the scarf and all that money. I got down into the bazaar and began walking very quickly. Then behind me I heard, 'Sahib! Sahib! You must come back! There has been a mistake!'

I kept walking but he soon caught up with me and began shouting to the bystanders in Hindi. Soon I was surrounded by an angry crowd. I was telling the merchant that we had done a deal to exchange the scarf and the £5 note and some rupees. He had made an offer and I had accepted it. He just kept shouting 'Money is like water,' which seemed to me irrelevant to the discussion. But the crowd that had gathered was hostile and the merchant was haranguing them in Hindi. I said I wanted to see a policeman. Eventually a cop came up with his stick, but he could speak no English and I am sure he was given a one-sided account of the affair. So we went to the police station, where a moustachioed old sergeant sat on the veranda. He listened to the case, then very wisely made everyone give everything back.

When I got back to Ron and told him how I had nearly been torn apart by an angry mob, he knew all about it – he had observed the whole thing. That bastard had stolen a handkerchief on our first visit, and then let me go there to change money without telling me. He thought the commotion had been all over the stolen handkerchief. And he just stood there watching. You know those Dutch that speak with an American accent? One of them.

I made it back to the Crown Hotel in Old Delhi where a German junkie lay on a bed all day, shooting opium and occasionally calling down the stairwell, 'Hey man! One yogurt – two banaan.' He used to share this food with me. I had nothing. I was starving. All I had was the bag of grass I'd brought from Kathmandu. It was pretty good stuff and I took it up to New Delhi to sell to the tourists. Sharing a cab to the embassies with a very straight American couple, they told me they had been in India for a week and hadn't had a smoke. That takes some doing. I said, 'Your troubles are over. I've got some very fine grass from Kathmandu at ten rupees a *tola*,' and pulled out a handful from my bag. In fact the whole bag had cost just three Nepalese rupees which is nothing. The guy looked judiciously at my *tola* and then offered me eight rupees for it. 'Very astute,' I said as I gave him the deal. Maybe I could survive by doing this.

My subsequent attempts at dealing were less successful. I usually ended up getting stoned and giving away my merchandise. I was very hungry.

On the street outside the Crown Hotel was a chai wallah with a tub of milk tea over a fire. You could buy a glass of this tea for a couple of annas. The wallah had two long ladles and he would pour the tea back and forth between them, then fill the glass and chop off a chunk of the cream

48

that floated on the tea to top it off. It was delicious – sweet and milky – and it was a meal. I lived on this tea and the German's bananas. I was starving. By the time I got home I had lost a stone in weight.

CHAPTER 5

Back on Canvey, Irene and I were living on one of the council estates that were changing the Island into a new town. Nearby was a house where local ne'er-do-wells used to congregate – I remembered these people as yobs and hard nuts before I had gone to university, but now they were transformed by the alchemy of LSD into hippies – fairly dangerous hippies. Among them was a teenage Lew Lewis, later to find fame in the punk era with his inspired harmonica and chaotic behaviour. It was a good place to hang out and get stoned and pass the time and listen to Jimi Hendrix.

I was at this time determined to work seriously on my painting. I had learned to paint at school and had a flair for it, but I had no formal art training and needed to improve my technique. My head was full of images – landscapes seething with reptilian life, ziggurats and towers, slow processions of winged bulls with the heads of men all marching out of Babylon and down to the very swamp where jewelled crocodiles swim. And more, beyond thought and description. Most of this imagery came from LSD trips I had taken. Although they were pinpoint sharp and colourful in my memory, I had never seen such things depicted anywhere and I wanted to write down these hieroglyphics of my soul. It would take months and years of work before my technique was equal to the task. I painted and drew and lived in a world of my own fantasy, my clothes covered in paint.

We had a spare room in our council house and sometimes people would live there. One of these was Dave Higgs (later to form Eddie and the Hot Rods). He fell into terrible depressions and painted his room black. The only variation was the black windows painted on the white door of the room which gave the impression of a Stygian night outside. Once he said to me, 'Can you get a black lightbulb?'

I painted and practised drawing and contemplated my visions and passed my time with Irene. Irene was working as a typist. But I needed a job and at the end of the year my mother, an infant-school teacher, found a vacancy for me as an English teacher at a local comprehensive school. At that time it was still possible to teach in schools without a teacher-training qualification if you had a university degree. I think they were pretty desperate for teachers there (two had left with nervous breakdowns during that first term) and the headmaster, obviously less than pleased with my long hair and scuzzy clothes, said he would give me a term's trial before confirming the job.

That very same day I met an old acquaintance on the street. Lee Collinson. I hadn't seen him for a couple of years.

I looked like a hippy with my long hair and paint-spattered clothes. Not so Lee. Here he came walking down the street towards me looking great – he was wearing a sharp pin-striped suit and his hair was cut short with sideburns. He was a nineteen-year-old solicitor's clerk – to me he looked like a star.

His personality was still what I remembered – eager and urgent, and his conversation terse and witty. We stood and talked – I told him I had just got this teaching job – and he told me that his skiffle group had evolved into an R&B band and their guitarist had left. I hadn't played at all since I went to university, but I still had my Fender Telecaster guitar under the bed . . . However, our conversation passed by without either of us asking the obvious question. But I was absolutely intrigued by Lee and wondered why I hadn't suggested forming a band. Later that day John Sparks the bass player knocked on my door. He said, 'Do you want to join our band?' and I said, 'Yes.'

At our first rehearsal I announced, 'We've got to be just like Johnny Kidd and the Pirates.' We learned some songs, among them Johnny Kidd's version of Willy Perryman's 'Doctor Feelgood'. Lee and Sparko wanted to call the band Doctor Feelgood but I said, 'It's been used before.' (Willy Perryman had gone under the name of Dr Feelgood and the Interns.) Then I said, 'Oh well, nobody on Canvey Island is gonna know.'

So we called the band Doctor Feelgood.

I started my teaching job after Christmas. I enjoyed the work and got on well with the kids and I think I achieved

some good results, especially with the rowdier and less aca-
demically inclined classes. They made fun of my long hair
and habit of sitting cross-legged on the teacher's desk (this
was 1972, the era of mullets, tank tops and platform shoes
for kids, so who looked ridiculous? All of us probably). The
school inspectors gave me very good reports and I thought
my job was secure. But this was the early seventies and
the education system was a mess. Untrained and inexperienced as I was, I could only go with the flow. The teachers
generally seemed to dislike the kids, and there was some
resentment against me from the older teachers – perhaps
because my degree put me on a higher pay scale (about £25
a week).

I liked most of the kids and set about learning how to
teach without being an arsehole. For instance, if you are
confronted by an unruly class, the thing to do is not raise
your voice or shout but gradually speak quieter and quieter,
until they are intrigued by what you are saying and then
quieter and quieter until there is absolute silence in the room
and then say 'Thank you' and carry on teaching.

I discovered that the curriculum meant that my fourth-
year class were going to get through school without having
read any Shakespeare. I thought, 'They're not getting past
me without reading Shakespeare,' and I found time on
Friday afternoons to read *Macbeth* with them. *Macbeth* is
really good for this with its violence and witches and rapid
action, and they didn't have to answer any boring questions
or write anything after our readings. I know I turned some
of them on to the poetry.

And there was Dr Feelgood – Me and Lee and Sparko and

a character called Terry Howarth on the drums. He was a
few years older than us, a northerner who had just left the
army. We used to call him 'Bandsman Howarth'. We were
a typical local amateur band. We were less typical in the
music we were trying to play – this was the old-fashioned
rhythm and blues, the music of Chuck Berry, Bo Diddley
and the great bluesmen from Chicago – the stuff that had
inspired The Rolling Stones ten years before. Other local
bands were wearing frocks and singing about going to
Mars, or bib-and-brace overalls and platform shoes playing
plodding 'progressive' music. Gigs were fairly few and far
between and we were pretty amateurish, but Lee proved to
be a brilliant front man – he had a powerful and distinctive
voice and played great harmonica and slide guitar. He was a
natural showman. All the nervous tension of his personality
could be felt in his aggressive presence and violent movements on stage. I knew he was a star.

In February 1972 my mother was taken into hospital with
uterine cancer. I knew nothing about cancer and I fondly
imagined that the radiation therapy she was receiving was
going to cure her. After finishing teaching for the day,
I would go to the hospital to see her. She was fifty-six.
She had devoted her life to making a decent home for our
working-class family. She taught me socialism and atheism, which she believed in with moral certitude. She had
scrubbed floors to pay for our school uniforms. Now we
were grown up, and she had qualified as a teacher and was
ready to live a life of her own. And there she was lying on
a hospital bed, white-haired and emaciated, an old woman.

She was going to die, and I knew she was going to die, but I couldn't admit it, I couldn't say it – I couldn't say, 'I love you, Mum, and I want to thank you for all you did for me.' Instead I sat there talking fatuously about nothing.

I woke one morning with sunlight reflecting from deep snow outside. Malcolm came in and told me that Mum had died.

We were following her coffin into the crematorium when I thought, 'Why do they carry the dead feet first? That means her head is at this end of the coffin. She had white hair.'

On that thought of her white hair I broke down crying – by the time we were inside I was sobbing uncontrollably, I just had to let it go.

In the pulpit stood some hired clergyman mouthing platitudes about my mother, who he had never met. And I cried and cried – I could not stop.

I wondered how my mother (her name was Catherine, though my father always used to call her 'Bet') would have reacted to this clergyman, with her staunch atheism.

I was still crying my heart out when we came to the door to leave – the clergyman could see I needed special consolation so he said, 'Don't worry, she's now reunited with her husband.'

I thought, 'Blimey, if her atheism proves false and she meets him up there she's not gonna be very pleased.' I was still sobbing helplessly.

As we drove home, the last of the snow that had fallen on the night of her death was melting away.

CHAPTER 6

Lee's jug band friend Chris Fenwick reappeared – in fact he rushed into our house one evening and ate my dinner. He had been in Holland and found some gigs for us, and he said he would buy a van and be our manager. The gigs fell during the school holidays, so they were good for me, but Bandsman Howarth was finding life in Civvy Street too difficult and went back into the army. We needed a drummer. I immediately suggested my old friend Johnny Martin. He had been working professionally with pop harmony bands, but I knew he was a good drummer. So The Big Figure joined Dr Feelgood, and the firm was complete.

The gigs in Holland were pretty good – Figure's drumming made the band much more powerful and we played to enthusiastic teenage audiences rather than in the dreary pubs we'd been playing at home. I started to think I would like to do this for a living.

During this tour we had some photographs taken at Den Bosch – one at the feet of the statue of Hieronymus Bosch, and another standing by some water. The second of these pictures survives and has amused generations of Dr Feelgood fans. There we all are in 1972, standing in a line, Lee in front in a denim jacket, me behind him, at his shoulder (I'm wearing a leather dustman's jacket with longish hair), and Sparko and Figure. A solicitor's clerk, a schoolteacher, a bricklayer and a drummer. An amateur band. But standing in front is Lee, and despite the denim, you can tell that he's the star. He always looked like a star. And this was a time of unalloyed happiness, before we set out on our road to eventual destruction. We were all good friends.

We went back to Holland for another little tour during the Easter holidays. I remember, on the ferry back home, I was trying to persuade Lee to go professional. Lee was talking about carrying on to get his law qualifications, and I was saying, 'Look, man, you're nineteen years old – you've got eternity in front of you for law exams. Right now you've got to seize the moment.'

Because I knew by now that, amateurish though we were, there was something special about Dr Feelgood.

I spent the rest of that Easter holiday marking schoolbooks – this was very important work for the fifth years' CSE exam and had to be completed for the first day of term. I returned to school to find that not one other member of staff had done the work. Not even the head of department.

I was now very unpopular with the headmaster, we just didn't get along. I was doing my job well – the inspectors had been in to see me a couple of times and given me very good reports – but he didn't like me. At the end of my first term he sent for me. I thought he was going to confirm my position, but instead he assumed a very serious and intelligent expression and said, 'I'm going to say something to you that I haven't had to say to a teacher in twenty years. You've got to do something about your appearance.' He wanted me to cut my hair.

I was taken by surprise. 'Once it was the Trotskyites,' I thought, 'and now it's you!' I said that when I'd been offered the job he'd said he wanted the school to nurture the individual – now he wanted me to adopt a uniform.

He slammed his hand on the desk and shouted, 'Dammit, boy, people think you're a student!'

I said, 'Don't call me boy. I'm not a boy. I've been around the world and I've read a lot of books and I'm not a boy. When do you want me to leave – now or at the end of term?'

I walked out of there shaking with fury. I knew I'd been doing good work and I didn't look that freaky – just like a student, apparently. I met a member of the English staff and told her what had happened. We realised that, being used to submissiveness at all times, the headmaster hadn't been expecting such a reaction – he actually thought I would obey his orders and cut my hair. What was more, he could ill afford to lose another member of staff.

I got home storming and raging to Irene, swearing I would never set foot in that school again. But this would have meant yet another change of teacher for my fifth-year class, who were coming up to exams. I couldn't desert them.

The next day was one of those training days they have

where all the local teachers gather at a certain school for lectures and so on. It so happened that this time the gathering was being held at my school. My brother was there – he was another long-haired person who taught locally – and we hooked up with a freak art teacher from Fred's Academy. We caused a bit of a stir as we walked around together, sniggering at the bone-headed drug lectures, and actually contributing useful opinions to the debates. Then came a moment when I was walking alone down a corridor and I came face to face with the headmaster. He came up to me, put his arm round my shoulder and said, 'About yesterday – shall we forget all about it?'

So I didn't desert my fifth years, but obviously my time wasn't going to last long. I resigned at the end of the summer term to become a professional musician.

'Going professional' was usually slang for being on the dole, but professional status was very important to me. I never claimed unemployment benefits, but subsisted on the £4 or £5 a week I could earn from playing.

We had a few regular gigs round Southend. The music we were playing was not fashionable and even Southend's Teddy boys were suspicious of us – we were not playing note for note covers of Eddie Cochran, Chuck Berry or Bill Haley. There were a few bands that catered to this archaic taste, but we weren't one of them. Once though, there was a cancellation and we were booked to play the Teddy boys' place – the Long Bar. The Teds were antagonistic from the start – we weren't wearing drape jackets and we were playing more R&B than rock 'n' roll. The crowd were getting ugly, shouting at us and waving feeble V signs. Suddenly, Lee was inspired by anger – he began singing and acting in a direct affront to these Teddy boys – he was threatening them – he was improvising lyrics – 'I'm gonna get back home, I'm gonna roll myself a joint, and I'm gonna laugh at all you cunts.' Not poetry, but it made its point. I stood beside Lee and joined him in taunting the crowd. It felt great – a real adrenaline rush – like just before a fight.

The gig continued as an angry confrontation. When we had finished there was a logistical problem. The Long Bar was aptly named and the stage was at the far end from the door. The space in between was crowded with Teddy boys who continued to abuse us. We had to pack up our equipment and get out. What did we do in the face of this threat? We packed our equipment, picked it up and carried it through the Long Bar to the door. The Teds parted like the Red Sea.

We already had some experience of Teddy boys. We used to get gigs backing Heinz, a one-hit wonder from the sixties with the Joe Meek song 'Just Like Eddie' who now sold advertising space for a local newspaper. Before he ended up with Dr Feelgood, Heinz had been a protégé of the eccentric producer of hits like 'Telstar', and his band in the sixties had included Ritchie Blackmore on guitar. Jimmy Page had played on his one hit, and he had appeared in the film *Live It Up* with Steve Marriott. So he'd worked with a lot of people.

Joe Meek had ended his own life with a shotgun after shooting his landlady dead. Heinz once said to me, 'The thing is – it was my fucking shotgun.'

Heinz used to play occasional gigs at Teddy-boy clubs, air-force bases and the like. We could earn more backing him than we could in our own right, and so that was what we did, whenever we could. We would pick him up in our van at a café outside Southend where he hid his car to deceive his employers about taking a day off.

We would usually open these gigs as Dr Feelgood, with Lee singing. We would keep it very rock 'n' roll, and then we would introduce ... The Dynamic Heinz! He would stumble on, wearing a sparkly drape suit, and begin to sing 'C'mon Everybody'. He would be drunk – he was like a fighter after ten rounds. There was a microphone on a stand and Lee and Chris got round it to do backing vocals. In those pre-monitor days it was impossible to hear the vocal mics from the stage and instead of singing 'Bop-shoo-wop' they would sing, 'Heinz bakes the meanest beans'. Heinz meanwhile would stagger drunkenly round the stage, his voice reduced to a hoarse whisper.

After the gig we would cart him back to the café where he had his car. There would then be drunken mumbling from the floor of the van – 'Ah! All those fucking barley wines!' and 'Juicy old crate, innit?' – as Chris clipped him for the petrol money.

In an attempt to make us look more Teddy-boy friendly, Heinz bought us some shirts to wear on stage. My shirt was red and black and I took to wearing it regularly – with a black suit. In 1974, when we were getting very busy I decided that my 'Irene' Telecaster was too precious to take on the road, so I bought a second-hand Telecaster of the same vintage (1962), sprayed it black and had a red scratch plate made for it, so that the guitar matched my shirt. This red and black Telecaster looked very distinctive and became associated with me as part of my stage image. You can now buy an official Fender 'Wilko Johnson' Telecaster in red and black – all those years after scraping pennies together and raiding Irene's savings to buy my first Telecaster, Fender have granted me this accolade. And it all began with Heinz's red and black shirt.

In August 1972, there was a great show at Wembley Stadium featuring Chuck Berry, Jerry Lee Lewis, Little Richard, Bo Diddley and Bill Haley, among others. And one of those others was Dr Feelgood. We were again there to provide a backing band for Heinz, who was due to open the show – so, thanks to Heinz, we were about to perform on stage at Wembley instead of the small local venues we were used to. I can remember almost shivering with nerves as we drove towards the twin towers of the stadium. It was fairly nerve-racking being up on that stage while Heinz made a pig's ear of some Eddie Cochran numbers – especially when he threw an inept karate kick in my direction and put every one of my strings out of tune – but feeling the music and the thrill of standing on a big stage in front of a huge audience, I was thinking, 'This is weird – a few days ago I was a schoolteacher and now I'm standing up here like a real musician. It feels good.'

Part of the art of backing Heinz was keeping up with his mistakes – if he went into a chorus too early or too late we were usually right with him. This was an important part of our value to him as a backing band. Up on that Wembley stage, though, the monitors weren't working and you couldn't hear Heinz's vocals. We didn't know where he was, but we forged along behind him, kicked-out strings and all. Despite all the difficulties it felt good – powerful – playing on that big stage. I wanted to do more.

When I came offstage and down to the dressing rooms below I saw Chuck Berry sitting in an electric-blue Rolls-Royce. I ran up to him with my guitar and asked him to sign it. He did so with a big smile. That evening he played one of the greatest shows I have ever seen.

Down in the dressing room, I heard another band begin to play. I thought it must be the first of the American acts and I walked outside to see. Onstage was Rock 'n' Roll – a singer with a wild Afro, a rhythm guitarist done up like the Silver Surfer and a lead guitarist all in black, his face painted gold like Tutankhamun. It looked really freaky. The guy was doing James Brown slides across the stage and singing 'Rambling Rose' in a high falsetto. They were laying down a big beat. This was the MC5 – I had heard some of their records, but now I was riveted by their live performance.

Not so the Teddy boys who made up a large part of the audience. They didn't like this psychedelic spectacle and were booing and throwing beer cans at the stage. The band played on – at one point the guitarist was moving across the stage and he kicked a beer can back into the crowd without even breaking his stride, and I just dug it more and more.

Back in the dressing room I saw the guitarist – his name, of course, is Wayne Kramer – and told him how much I had dug the show, and apologised for the bad reception they had been given. I tried to explain about Teddy boys and how they believed that rock 'n' roll was something that happened in the fifties and shouldn't be changed in any way. (It amused me later that night to see them bopping furiously while Chuck Berry added lyrics about rolling joints and stuff to his songs.)

Anyway, I left Wayne Kramer looking pretty gloomy. They may have had a bad time with this English audience, but that show changed my life.

After seeing the MC5 I began to realise the importance of physical action and dynamics in playing rock 'n' roll. Lee's stage presence was already impressively frantic, but now I started to react to him and try to move like I had seen Wayne Kramer do on stage. I even did a couple of gigs with my face painted gold.

CHAPTER 7

One evening in 1973, I went to a phone box and called the hospital. A nurse told me, 'Your wife has given birth to a baby boy.' I was dancing in the middle of the street when a police car pulled up. I said to the cops, 'It's a boy!' They congratulated me and left me dancing. I don't think you can get much happier than that.

After Mum died, we had moved into the little bungalow where we grew up – Malcolm and his then wife Annie, me, Irene and baby Matthew. I remember watching Irene the first time she took him out in his pram. It was one of those old-fashioned prams with a fringed awning – it looked like a galleon in full sail, and Irene behind it looking so proud and self-conscious. And I remember a couple of years later Matthew looking up at me with a puzzled expression on his face when I returned from a six-week tour of America.

That was a happy home. The very same place that had

once been blighted by my father's presence was now a place of sunshine and laughter.

When the *OZ* obscenity trial happened, Malcolm and I were outraged by the draconian sentencing of the editors and decided to take action. One night we took a bucket of blue paint and a brush and went to the brick gable end of a local shop and painted in large dribbling blue letters: OZ NOW YOU NEXT. Now this was fairly incomprehensible even when we did it, and as time went by it became positively gnomic, but there it remained, in the centre of Canvey Island, right outside the school gates, for many years. Generations of schoolkids walked past it every day. Once I was on Canvey with some Japanese rock 'n' roll tourists, and they wanted to photograph this graffiti. The school was coming out as we did this and I asked a bunch of girls if they had the slightest idea what it meant – of course they didn't – it means absolutely nothing, and yet there it had stood for decades. It's been painted over now (and replaced by really grotty 'tags') but it is commemorated on a tourist plaque in the park on Canvey Island as 'the famous graffiti'. (Malcolm and I are not credited.)

This was not the only agit-prop activity we got involved in. It was proposed to build two massive new oil refineries, covering the western half of Canvey Island. Local people were alarmed – Canvey Island was becoming a new town and many people from the East End of London and beyond had bought homes, seeing it as an idyllic alternative to Dagenham and Walthamstow. Now the value of their homes was to be destroyed and the nature of Canvey Island corrupted by this decision, without local consultation, from above. They were going to open a big new road on to Canvey – a road which was to provide easy access to the island for oil tankers – and a demonstration was planned for the opening ceremony.

Malcolm and I got there to find a confused scene – a stage had been erected next to a white ribbon stretched across the road – no doubt in readiness for some fatuous ritual involving giant scissors, and a small crowd was gathering. It was the middle of a weekday and the crowd consisted mostly of housewives. There were mothers and children.

And there were police. There had never been such a thing as a demonstration on Canvey Island before and the police had massively overreacted. Apart from the fact that the numbers of police almost equalled those of the crowd, they had got hold of a huge vehicle-lifting lorry (to stop people blocking the highway with their cars – though there were no cars), and many other police cars and vans. The demonstrators were as inexperienced and confused as the police, so Malcolm and I called to them to go to the stage and heckle the dignitaries standing there. You can just imagine Mr Plod watching us lead the straggling crowd to the podium and encourage them to shout protests at the Mayor – 'Long-haired anarchist agitators!' In fact our protests were very restrained and civilised – as I said, everybody was inexperienced, and there were children present, so we were hardly storming the Bastille.

Nevertheless the police had invested huge resources in this operation and needed a result, so I was arrested mid-slogan and taken to the police cell at Benfleet to be followed fifteen minutes later by a very flustered Malcolm. We were charged with threatening behaviour, obstructing the police and obstructing the highway. People at the demonstration were outraged at the arbitrary behaviour of the police and a meeting was called on Canvey Island the next day. Thus was formed the Canvey Island Oil Refineries Resistance Group.

The Resistance Group attracted wide support on Canvey Island, holding demonstrations and meetings. It was one of the first of the environmental protest groups that were to become so widespread in the seventies. We picketed the oil refinery construction site, trying to persuade lorry drivers not to deliver material, and we searched for publicity.

Once we drove two coachloads of mothers and children to London to the offices of the Italian company that was building one of the refineries. It was in that gothic-style edifice you see at the end of Park Lane.

A couple of us went and told security that we had come from Canvey Island to make a complaint. They obligingly stood aside and we decanted all the mothers and children into the office, where they took the place over. We put our banners outside on the balcony and called the TV news.

The police arrived, but they took no action as we were behaving in a lawful manner and causing no damage – a copper just stood at the door and watched all these kids running around disrupting the office routine. We were shown on the TV news that evening, as well as reported in the evening papers.

The protest movement went from strength to strength, even going into 10 Downing Street to deliver a petition, and meeting some very powerful people, but of course it did no good – these refineries were 'essential' for the economy and building went ahead. Then there was some crisis in the international oil market and the refineries were no longer essential – in fact they were abandoned, leaving nothing but a huge chimney, a truly massive and never-used jetty and some rusty tanks, and almost leaving me with a criminal record – I had been found guilty of obstructing the highway, even though I was arrested before the big scissors cut the white ribbon. I won the appeal.

There was a documentary series on BBC TV called *Man Alive* and they devoted an episode of this to the Canvey Island Oil Refineries Resistance campaign. You can see me on this programme with my very long hair confounding some economist in a debate. It was my first TV appearance. When I saw it, I thought, 'It's really time to get a haircut!', so maybe *Man Alive* played its part in the development of Dr Feelgood.

And of course the irony wasn't lost on me that I should be protesting so vigorously against the building of these refineries when I had loved Shell Haven all my life, and when Dr Feelgood were spending so much time fantasising about and glorifying what we had come to know as 'Oil City'.

CHAPTER 8

We got a residency playing every week at the Cloud Nine discotheque on Canvey Island, and we had a few other regular gigs around Southend, but most of the time we were hanging out, getting stoned and laughing. Lee could be hysterically funny. The more splenetic he became, the funnier it got. He would talk about people in rival bands with malicious glee and give them names – Coypu on guitar, Moth on drums, Wallaby on bass – which were extraordinarily apt. (Once we were out driving and we passed by this perfectly respectable guy standing at a bus stop. Somebody said, 'Who's that?' and Lee said in a judicious voice, 'Roonsel Poozle.' And this perfectly respectable guy, with his pin-stripes and umbrella, was transformed by Lee's ludicrous baptism into a figure of utter ridicule. It was the way he said it – you had to be there.) He would go into raps that could become frenzied or deeply illogical, or routines like 'Larry the Penis', always very funny.

Sparko was a stoical, unflappable character with a cynical grin and a great talent for sleeping. He could fall asleep anywhere – he told me that one morning he had been setting out for work when he had opened the boot of his Jaguar and seen some cosy-looking blankets in there. Half an hour later his friends had found him sound asleep with his legs hanging out of the back of the car. He had a laconic, building-site wit and was a master of obscenity. And he really was unflappable, seeming to take his whole life at an ambling pace – I once did a day's hod-carrying for him and I was easily able to keep up with his leisurely bricklaying.

Figure would laugh till he couldn't breathe, holding on to the wall with both hands. (Figure, my oldest friend. He is a good-hearted fellow – there is no malice in him.) During these times we would sometimes fantasise about being in a big band and riding in a Cadillac. This was before the advent of *The Blues Brothers*, but that's the kind of thing.

We adopted stage names – 'The Big Figure' already had his name, Lee took himself to New Orleans by adopting 'Brilleaux' instead of Collinson, and I, with syllabic dexterity, became Wilko Johnson. I changed my name by deed poll. I was finally rid of my father. It's on my passport, it's what my family and friends have always called me, and anybody who tries to ingratiate themselves by addressing me as 'John' really annoys me. I'm Wilko.

Once we had a gig at Durham University and drove up there in our dilapidated old van. The gig was some kind of student celebration and the ballroom was packed with people in fancy dress. We entered into the spirit of the thing. Even I, a puritanical teetotaller, indulged in a glass or two of Scotch, which led me to a window where I could look down on the River Wear. Waves of sentimental nostalgia for university days washed through me. I felt a kind of sad envy for these partying students. Here I was, a musician at their party, I must seem like some figure from another world. But really I was an ex-student and I felt more in common with them than I did with the world of rock 'n' roll. It takes a while before you think of yourself as a musician and not Joe Bloggs who happens to be playing in a band. When you talk to people it feels like you're pretending. Then, once you've been in it for a couple of years, you can say it – 'I'm a musician.' Because you are.

Anyway, it was a good party gig. A streaker ran across the stage while we were playing. Lee nicked the jacket from his pile of discarded clothes, and wore it for some time after-wards – perhaps it played its part in creating the Feelgood style.

We slept the night on the floor of the student union and set off for home in the morning in very good spirits. Sparko, who had entered into the party spirit very freely the night before, suddenly rolled down the window and puked into the wind. Then, without wiping his mouth, he turned round to me and said, 'Give us a kiss!' And so the merry miles rolled by – until the engine took sick, coughed, spluttered and finally died. We pulled over to the side of the road, climbed up the embankment and sat down. Sitting there in the sun watching the traffic go by, I felt so happy and free. The band was startling audiences wherever we went. I was a musician. Irene and the baby were at home – the best was yet to come. Just sitting there in the sun.

If I could buy that feeling now . . .

Eventually Lee and Chris walked off across the fields. Time went by. When you're winning, things just go your way – I knew that we would find our way back home. Lee and Chris returned, driving up in a van they had rented with God knows what mendacity, and we loaded all our equipment from the old van into the new one. Fortunately we had a length of rope, and I sat with Figure in our old van as we were towed along the A1. Figure had been chosen to drive the old van as he was an expert driver, and there's an art to being towed on an old piece of rope. If the rope goes slack and then tightens up it will break, so when it does go slack, skilful use of the brake and accelerator is required. Despite Figure's skills, eventually the rope pulled tight and broke. The others had to drive on to the next roundabout to turn round and rescue us. Using a half-sheepshank, double granny knot, we tied the broken ends of our tow rope together and carried on down the road. And I felt so good.

After a while the rope broke again, and the others, all unaware, drove off into the distance. When they got back to us we tied the rope with the strongest knot we could manage. So we had two knots and the rope was getting shorter – the vans were almost bumper to bumper as we approached Aylesbury. In the end the rope broke yet again and now it was useless, but I was feeling good and I knew that things were bound to go our way. A short distance from the road there was a clump of trees. I walked across to them and I found what I had expected: there was a rope hanging from a sturdy branch, a children's swing. I climbed the tree and untied the rope and carried it triumphantly back feeling good.

It was growing dark. Our new tow rope was faultless as

we drove along the road to Canvey Island. Nothing could stop us. Then a tyre blew on our old van. So near to home, we were stranded. Sparko told us he knew of a thing – it was an aerosol foam that could inflate a burst tyre. They drove off to Canvey, leaving me and Figure in the van. It was cold and dark. Here's their headlights, they came driving back. And do you know what – that aerosol really worked and we got home to Canvey. When you're winning, everything goes your way.

CHAPTER 9

I started writing songs. I had never really considered song-writing in the early days of the band – we were still playing covers of American rock 'n' roll and R&B songs from the fifties and sixties, and this was a vast resource of material, from Chuck Berry's classic hits to the more obscure stuff on the Chess Records label. There were hundreds of great songs to be found in that style, hardly any of them being played by bands in the seventies, so we didn't lack for a distinctive repertoire. If ever the idea of writing original material occurred to me, I would dismiss it, thinking, 'Who needs original material when all this great unplayed stuff exists?' Besides, I didn't think I had the gift of song-writing – in all the time I had been playing, I had never written a song, and when I listened to Mickey Jupp's *Red Boot* album, which was full of brilliant, powerful R&B-style songs, I was intimidated. I thought songwriting was for the few who had been born with such a talent, and not for me.

But as the band got better and started finding a style of its own, with my 'Mick Green' guitar and Lee's voice growing more powerful and distinctive, I began to try and write. My first attempts produced a couple of fairly lightweight pop songs, which we recorded in a little studio (well, a shed with a tape recorder in it) in Southend. I remember going into that studio – I was very, very nervous – but at the end of the day, we had recorded four songs: two covers (Johnny Kidd and the Pirates' 'I Can Tell' and 'Checkin' Up On My Baby' by Sonny Boy Williamson) and my two efforts. Listening to these recordings later, I realised that my songs, although somewhat naive, stood up for themselves. People would hear our tape and draw no distinction between the covers and my songs – some people even expressed a preference for mine. We started playing the songs in our live set, and found that they went down well with audiences. I told Lee never to tell audiences that these songs were original, so we could get an unprejudiced reaction when they were played alongside the classics that made up most of our set. So my confidence grew – songwriting wasn't some Cabalistic art, gifted at birth – anyone could do it if they had a feel for the music they were playing.

I had come up with a riff which worked in my lead/ rhythm guitar style. It was a simple, repeated lick inside a fast rock 'n' roll rhythm – you could play it on the guitar unaccompanied and it just went driving along. I had written some conventional verses (praising 'that woman' – actually Irene in my mind) and I needed a hook or chorus to hang them on – four syllables, *da, da, da, DA*, to sum it up. My first thought was 'She's Outta Sight', but I couldn't use this – not only was it clichéd but it was an American idiom. I wanted my lyrics to be in a vernacular suited to the Thames Estuary – I wanted Lee to sing the way he would have spoken. Four syllables of doggerel verse. It's not Shakespeare, but it wasn't easy to find. I paced round and round the room going, 'She out of sight – No! – She something else – No! – She this and that – No! – She dum dum dum . . . ' Round and round the room. Four syllables.

I thought of Sir Philip Sidney, *biting my truant pen, beating myself for spite* – '*Fool*', said my muse to me – '*look in thy heart and write*'. I looked in my heart and I couldn't find it there. Round and round the room, getting more and more frustrated. Four bloody syllables! 'She what what what – She she she she . . . ' I was nearly beating myself for spite when there it was – 'She does it right' – and the whole simple little song was there. I could imagine Lee delivering this lyric with real conviction, while the band would blast out my simple riff behind him. Sparko had a style of bass riffing which he called 'knocking on', and it fitted perfectly with my guitar riff to give a real driving effect. 'She Does It Right' was my first real Dr Feelgood song.

I had another, slightly more complicated riff that I set about making a song out of. Again, I wanted a 'Thames Estuary' lyric, and I took it right down to Canvey Island with the phrase *Down by the jetty* for the chorus, opening the song with a picture of my beloved refinery – *Stand and watch the towers burning at the break of day*. Then it was a matter of finding images of urban confusion for the verse – *Streets are full of signs, arrows pointing everywhere.* This lyric came much more easily than the first. I was finding a method, and that method consisted of inventing a guitar riff – something I could do in my head, or twanging on my guitar – and then seeing what it suggested. All riffs, when you listen to them, seem to express a certain feeling – happy, angry, silly or whatever – and this tells you what to write about. Some riffs almost seem to speak words.

But the song doesn't always come from the riff. One time I was listening to a Coasters record – 'Turtle Dovin' – which had a doo-wop vocal backing. I was really enjoying this and decided I'd like to write such a song. I started off going 'Sha doo dah wop bop bop, Sha doo dah wop bop bop,' and wrote a silly lyric about a cheating woman to go over it – *I saw you out the other night/I saw somebody hold you tight.* Then I needed the woman's name, so I could accuse her. Now this name needed two syllables – 'Dum DUM' – and again I found myself walking round the room trying to find a simple phrase. And I can't find it and I can't find it. It was a silly song and I wanted a silly name – a name of two syllables.

Eventually I decided to invent a name for this wanton woman and I came up with 'Roxette'. (The name was later adopted by the Swedish band Roxette, who had several very big hits in the eighties, as well as by untold hundreds of dogs and cats, and a few unfortunate human beings who have been given the name – but *I* invented it, for this throwaway song.)

Anyway the song was written, and performed, over the *Sha doo dah wop bop bop* vocal backing. It was only when

78

we got into a recording studio that I thought of a guitar riff to replace the vocal backing and suddenly the song became a real Dr Feelgood thing – in fact it sounded so right it became our first single and eventually one of Dr Feelgood's best-loved songs. So, it ain't always the riff that comes first.

Names are funny things. When you first write a song it's difficult to refer to it by its title, like when you have a new baby and you can't refer to him as 'Timmy' – you call him 'the baby'. And so with songs – it's either 'that shuffle' or 'that one in A' until you get used to it.

I soon became adept at writing songs for Dr Feelgood. I would write them with Lee's voice in my mind, both in sound and vocabulary. The melodies and chord changes would always conform to rhythm and blues patterns – they never strayed far from the basic twelve-bar blues. What is it about the twelve-bar blues? It is so satisfying and infinitely useful. Like the sonnet in poetry, it's a simple, recognised shape that can be used over and over again for different songs. Variants of this chord sequence form the basis of most of my songs. I usually adapt it in some way, rather than using the straightforward pattern, but I never stray far from it I just like it.

Everything from 'Johnny B. Goode' to 'The St Louis Blues' to a thousand other songs uses this sequence. Who invented it? Same bloke who invented the sonnet probably.

And lyrics can be hard to find – you scratch your head all night to get some words to fit a riff. But sometimes a lot of syllables can come out of nowhere. We used to play 'Great Balls Of Fire' in our live set and I thought it would be good to replace this old chestnut with an original song. I sat down and played the riff we used for 'Great Balls Of Fire' and almost immediately came out with this extended medical/sexual double-entendre to fit over it:

You Shouldn't Call The Doctor

Girls if your heart is feeling sore
Call the doctor and I'll fix it for sure
I'll be over right away, but you might find you have to
    pay
For a private consultation and a guaranteed cure

When you're dying of a dreadful disease
You don't worry 'bout the medical fees
And it's too late to change your mind, the doctor's pulling
    down the blind
And your temperature is rising to a hundred degrees

I'll cuddle up beside you for a start
And listen to the beating of your heart
And then I'll take you gently by the hand
And ask you when the trouble first began
And then I'll look down deep into your eyes
And if your temperature continues to rise
There's only one way to make it stop
I'll have to prescribe the strongest medicine I've got

And if this doesn't cure you it'll kill
But I know it's gonna give you a thrill

And now I've come across you can't complain about the
   cost
You shouldn't call the doctor if you can't afford the bills.

Just like that, written in five or six minutes on one page of my notebook.

Other times lyrics or parts of lyrics can elude you for months, and rough drafts and crossings-out fill up reams of paper. Sometimes you can have a lyric and not know it – when I wrote 'Sneaking Suspicion', I remember telling Figure that I had written a song, but couldn't think of a good chorus or title line, so I had used 'Sneaking Suspicion' as a temporary measure. When the producer Bert DeCouteaux identified the song as a 'million-seller', he remarked on the title as one of its assets, and it was used as the title track for the Feelgoods' fourth album.

So I went on writing these things, and we played them unannounced, and they fitted right in with the older classics we were playing.

One of the most flattering reviews I got in the early days was one that said Dr Feelgood were a great band, but they needed some original material – the reviewer had assumed that my songs were classics like the rest of our set.

CHAPTER 10

We heard about the London pub rock scene. This was a circuit of venues devoted to live music, with good bands playing and an audience that was there for the music rather than just the beer. There were established places like the Marquee and the 100 Club, as well as new venues like Dingwall's, and pubs like the Hope & Anchor. Many of the musicians playing these gigs were well known, and playing all kinds of stuff – rock, country, jazz-rock, comical, historical, pastoral – but they were often clad in denim and stood with their backs to the audience or looked at their shoes. There was a lot of good music, but most of it was kind of tame. We went up to London to see some of these gigs and the bands that were playing there, with the idea of getting some work for ourselves.

Once we had checked out the opposition, I felt pretty confident that there was nothing to touch us. I must make an exception here for Kilburn & the High Roads – led by Ian Dury with his brilliant lyrics and stage presence, they presented what can only be described as a spectacle. Limping on to the stage came Ian, crippled by polio and dressed as his hero Gene Vincent – a big black guy, also crippled, took the drums – the lanky Humphrey Ocean (later to find fame as an artist – I remember a conversation with Humphrey telling me he was giving up rock 'n' roll to concentrate on painting – this gave me a pang and I told him I envied him – oh well); then there was crazy Davey Payne on sax. Altogether they were a pretty formidable crew, but Ian's time was yet to come and right now the moment was ours.

When Dr Feelgood came to town we had the look, the stage show – which was now a double act between me and Lee (he would be the gang leader and I his lieutenant with a gun) – and our straight-ahead rock 'n' roll. We were all new faces, and our short hair and suits and violent stage show set us apart from the other bands. Soon we were packing venues all over London and getting good reviews in the music press. I remember standing outside the Kensington once before a gig when a cab full of people pulled up. I thought, 'Wow, we must be getting really famous. People who can afford to ride in taxis are coming to our gigs!' There were young people in our audiences who liked the excitement of our shows and saw that rock 'n' roll could be made with minimal equipment and a lot of physical energy, rather than multi-keyboard, multi-electronic effects set-ups. Many of these people went on to form the punk bands of 1976. We had a devoted following and we were attracting attention from the mainstream music business, and more. It began to look like something big was going to happen.

One night we were travelling home after a very good gig. It had been full of people from the music biz – A&R men, journalists, etc. – and some extravagant offers were being made. As we drove over the flyover at Barking, with the lights of Essex spread out around us, I said, 'I wonder what's gonna happen.' The whole world lay before us as we rode over that flyover.

I went out into the fields on Canvey Island one day and thought about my painting. If I was going to devote myself seriously to music I would never be able to learn to paint properly. What was it to be? Starve in a garret creating works of art, or ride in a Cadillac and get all the girls? I gave up painting.

We carried on playing the London scene. Every Saturday night we played at the Kensington, a crazy set-up where the stage was in the passageway between two bars and the band played facing people squashed against the wall, while most of the audience was in the bars to either side. There was a real danger of jabbing people in the face with my guitar as I moved across the stage, and sometimes I would have to apologise as I came flying back the other way. The place used to get packed to overflowing and we would finish our set soaked in sweat while the crowd went wild. With this and other gigs like Dingwall's and the Marquee and good press in all the music papers, especially the *NME*, we had become the hottest thing in town.

We also started playing further afield to new audiences in towns and colleges round the UK. We went down well with people who saw us for the first time – the initial reaction was often one of surprise or shock, and then you would see people smile – they had got the joke – it's very easy to understand – and away we went. Once a bloke came up to me after one of these gigs obviously very excited by the show, and said, 'You're the best semi-professional guitarist I've ever seen!' – a back-handed compliment I have always cherished.

Although we were making such an impact with our live shows, the record companies were cautious – they didn't know if a very basic club act like ours could translate into big record sales. But I knew that we could play big venues, where big stages and lights and larger auditoriums would give our show the space it needed; the stages in the club gigs were necessarily small, and the lighting and PA inadequate to show the band to full effect. So we carried on playing on those small stages, coming offstage, soaked in sweat, into dressing rooms that were nothing more than toilets or kitchens or dusty corridors behind the stage stacked with old chairs; but we always gave everything we'd got, no matter how humble the circumstances. You might have an audience of just a couple of dozen but you wanted every one of them to walk away excited by the show they'd seen, and Dr Feelgood soon gained a reputation for *always* giving a show of real kicks.

But we still didn't have a record deal. I grew very frustrated with the reluctance of the record companies and our failure to get signed. When, occasionally, another band on the pub rock scene got a deal, it would drive me crazy with jealousy.

Eventually, though, we got our deal, when Andrew Lauder signed us to United Artists. He was the one who gave us our break. UA was a subsidiary of the film company and occupied a single floor of their building in Mortimer Street. The record company was small, with just a few acts – Hawkwind and Man were their biggest. It was very groovy – there was a big office with a massive wooden table covered in graffiti and you could just go there and hang out, while Andrew and his staff did their work around you. It was a good place to be, with different musicians turning up to pass the time. Lemmy, then Hawkwind's bass player, often dropped in, until he was banned for removing too many records from the stock cupboard and taking them straight to the Camden record dealers. Of course there were always freebies available, but I think Lemmy was shifting them in industrial quantities.

UA got us some gigs supporting Hawkwind to give us experience of larger venues. These shows took us round the country to new audiences. When we played at Manchester City Hall, the audience, keen to see Hawkwind and their naked dancer Stacia, were restless with us – and some of them were actively hostile. They started booing. They started throwing pennies at the stage. Lee picked up one of these coins, bit it and threw it contemptuously to the floor. It was a real rush. Just like with the Teddy boys in the Long Bar, we were defying the audience and flying high – I knew we were winning. The next time we went to Manchester, at UMIST, we played to a sold-out and wildly enthusiastic audience.

With our first advance from United Artists we bought a coach and had it customised with beds and room to carry our equipment. It was good travelling in this coach – you could lie down and sleep, or walk up and down, and it often served as a dressing room outside club gigs.

One night, 21 November 1974, we had a gig in the middle of Birmingham, in New Street. We had just started playing when I saw blue lights in the street outside. The police came in and said that there had been a bombing and the place had to be evacuated. People left quickly and we were left behind, packing up our equipment. I stepped outside to find the street deserted. There were more blue lights flashing at the bottom of the hill and a terrible silence. A policeman came up and told us to check our coach before starting it. Lee got in the driver's seat and I sat beside him. 'If one goes, we both go.' He turned the ignition key – and the engine started normally.

It was clear that the bomb had been devastating, and that our families would be seeing it on TV, knowing that we were playing in New Street and with no way to contact us. We packed up as quickly as we could and drove to a telephone box to tell our families we were safe. The next day we broke into a furious argument on the coach – we were screaming and shouting at each other – but I think we were really screaming about what we'd seen the night before.

CHAPTER 11

We made our first album, *Down By The Jetty*, with producer Vic Maile. Multi-track recording had developed to a stage where studios looked like the flight deck on the starship *Enterprise* and records were made by recording the drums and bass first, overdubbing one, two or twenty guitar tracks and then throwing in the kitchen sink – people could play on records and never even meet the other musicians.

I didn't know anything about recording, but I did know that the records I loved had been recorded without overdubbing – you could hear one guitar, one drum kit, one bass, etc., all playing together. This was what I wanted to do – as far as possible, record the band live in the studio.

There was some resistance to this. Vic Maile wanted to produce the record in the conventional way using overdubbing and other studio tricks to make the sound 'commercial'. But I refused to do any overdubbing. There was only one guitar in Dr Feelgood, in fact my style was a percussive, choppy sound designed to work on its own. So why falsify our sound by smothering it with non-existent overdubbed instruments? The record company argued, but I insisted on keeping the recording simple and basic. We recorded all the tracks in one or two takes and used no overdubbing.

When it came to mixing this album there was a problem. How do you mix three instruments – drums, bass and guitar – into stereo? You've got to put the drums in the middle. You could then put the bass and guitar to either side, but this sounds wrong – the bass has got to be in the centre. This leaves the guitar stuck out to one side on its own, a completely false sound. The only answer I could see was to move the guitar too into the centre, creating a mono sound.

Some of the tracks had piano on them and these could be mixed in conventional stereo with the guitar and piano panned to either side, but then the record sounded inconsistent. The mono tracks sounded best so we mixed the stereo tracks into mono (i.e. we panned all the sounds on this stereo record into the centre). I asked the record company not to write the word *mono* on the sleeve – I didn't want Dr Feelgood to be regarded as some kind of retro thing and the word mono would set off all kinds of speculations. The record was in mono because it sounded best that way, not as some kind of statement. And I know that nobody on hearing the record would remark, 'Oh, it's in mono!' In fact, if the word hadn't been printed on the record sleeve, nobody would ever have known, but the company were muttering about the Trades Descriptions Act and I still have to answer questions about 'back to mono' forty years later. It doesn't matter. It's just a record.

The album sold moderately well (in time it would come to be regarded as a minor classic and regularly appear in lists of the '100 Greatest Albums') and we were touring bigger venues – city halls and theatres, and a couple of live TV appearances which caused quite a stir. Our shows were all sellouts and we seemed unstoppable. It felt like we held the zeitgeist in our hands.

With Irene and our little son Matthew, life was pretty good – domestic bliss at home and fame and flattery up in town. Heads would turn everywhere I went – it's impossible to remain aloof from this kind of attention – every slightest movement becomes a pose. It feels uncomfortable. The transition from obscurity to fame is a precipitate one and it takes a while to get used to people treating you like a star. You feel like saying, 'No, no – it's only me!'

By then our live gigs were something special. We had a fanatical young audience. Schoolkids were finding they could get real excitement at our shows, and it was easy to dress up as Dr Feelgood and escape for a while into our B-movie fantasy.

And it was great to be on stage with Lee – I always looked on him as the fount and origin of Dr Feelgood; it was his energy and passion that set the whole thing going.

Standing beside him on stage, I flick my head towards him, see him wiping sweat from his brow and glaring at the audience, tense as a fighter. He's the boss. On his nod I start to do my thing – that ain't a guitar, it's a tommy gun, and the audience erupts – then back beside him, ready to kill anyone he tells me to. It made you feel powerful, like no one could touch you.

A great thing about Dr Feelgood's gigs was they were always so good-time – there was never any trouble. All that aggression and gunplay from the stage was just a fantasy that everyone enjoyed. 'Riot In Cell Block Number Nine' wasn't a song about a riot, it was a picture of a B-movie riot, and we would act out that movie with total conviction, because we believed it too. And I'm firing my guitar gun and it's just like being a kid playing cops and robbers – your pointed fingers really are a gun and you really are firing it. That's the way we played our shows, and that's the way the crowd enjoyed them.

And that's the way that Lee was, as the front man of Dr Feelgood. I always admired Lee – although he was four years younger than me, from the very first he seemed to have a maturity and self-possession that made him a natural leader. I'm fairly shy, Lee was gregarious. He was very likeable and could talk to all kinds of people. I admired him, and I think he had respect for me. But we never told each other that. ('Oh, man, I rilly admire you!' – can you imagine it? We're from Canvey Island, for fuck's sake!) Maybe we should have. But Lee was the leader, and I liked it that way. Not only did I write those songs for him, with his voice in my head, but I followed his lead on stage. It all came down to Lee.

We got a gig at a festival in Avignon – a big Roman amphitheatre. We were touring the UK at the time and we needed to hire a plane to get there. It was pretty cool boarding this four-engined aircraft, getting into the air and then seeing a bloke up the front dressed as a pilot sniffing coke. These guys were a laugh – they would piss out of the doors and let us all have a go at flying. At the festival there were a lot of big names, but we weren't intimidated – we'd just got off our plane, and we knew we had that thing. The amphitheatre was huge and almost vertical, like people wallpaper, and the French crowd were hyped up for Dr Feelgood's first big appearance in France. We were stars.

We took to the stage at the very moment the sun went down and the atmosphere was magic. The sudden twilight and the colours of the sky. We gave a fierce performance and stole the show, walking off that stage to tumultuous cheers and applause. There was a pretty girl standing in the wings as we came offstage. I just beckoned to her and she came with me. Star.

Another time in France we were due to play a festival when we received a sudden offer to do some television filming. This meant we couldn't do the festival, so Chris went and told the organisers that we were ill, and off we went to the town for the filming. We shot a scene on the street where we had to go and ask directions from a girl in a big American car, then they filmed us running across some waste ground as though we were being pursued.

Then they told us that they wanted us to perform a few live numbers in a local schoolyard, so we went there and the crew were setting the equipment up. Chris arrived with an emergency – the promoters of the festival, who had been told we were ill, had turned up. What were we to do?

Chris said we should put on a good performance, since it was being filmed, but make it look like we were all a bit poorly. Meanwhile some nuns came into the schoolyard leading the whole school of junior kids, who sat cross-legged facing the stage. So, all we had to do was to perform a full-on rock 'n' roll show to an audience of eight-year-old kids in school uniform, while pretending to be ill. What the results of this filming were I don't know, but French friends have assured me it was shown on television.

Back at home I began writing songs for our next album. Despite my constant attempts to involve the others, especially Lee, in songwriting, they never made any efforts to join in and as a result songwriting was something I did alone. To them songs were something that came out of nowhere. They were never to be found pacing the room hunting for syllables or inventing new licks and riffs.

One night I was sitting talking to Irene when a catchy little chorus came into my head. The baby started crying, Irene went off to see to him and I started writing this song. I could tell it was a good one and, with my newly acquired tape recorder, I began putting it down, line by line. It was a long process as I wasn't familiar with the tape machine, but by the early hours of the morning I had recorded the whole song – backing, lead vocal, backing vocal and all. The song was called 'Back In The Night' and I was sure it was a hit.

There was a rehearsal booked for the morning so I took my tape recorder in my arms and, being a non-driver, carried the heavy machine over a mile to the studio. I was so excited by my night's work and I set up the machine and played the song for the first time.

'Well, what do you think?'

They looked at each other and hummed and ha'd and were generally underwhelmed. In fact they were right on the edge of sneering. Of course, they didn't know what it was to stay up all night writing a song, so they felt no need to be tactful. I knew it was a good song – it went on to become Dr Feelgood's best-known song all around the world – but to them it was a thing of no importance. I didn't say anything, but I was upset.

We made our second album, *Malpractice*, which included 'Back In The Night', along with numbers like 'Riot In Cell Block Number Nine' that were popular from our live shows. And a song called 'Going Back Home', which I had written over a killer riff that Mick Green had taught me. I took more of a back seat on this record – on *Down By The Jetty*, I had done everything from the recording to the sleeve design. The album was successful, and it was our first release in America.

Chris had built a house on Canvey – 'Feelgood House' – and parties there would be filled with rock people and journalists. The 'Thames Delta' became mythologised. Our origins in the strange backwater we called 'Oil City' added to our outlaw image, and, yes, we made Canvey Island famous, even more than the floods of 1953 had done. People still come from all over the world to make rock 'n' roll pilgrimages to Canvey Island.

*

In 1975 Led Zeppelin had been playing three nights at Earl's Court and Robert Plant had asked for Dr Feelgood to play at the after-gig party. We found ourselves confronted by an audience including the Atlantic Records establishment – Ahmet Ertegun, the lot. They seemed to enjoy what we were doing, but what were they thinking about four English guys playing music they had created fifteen years before? Much of our repertoire had originated on Atlantic Records. We drove to the after-party party to get our money. Pulling up in Chris's dad's battered old Merc beside all these gleaming limousines, we felt pretty cool and mean.

The Americans were interested by what they had seen of us at Zeppelin's party and Chris began to talk to them, eventually going to the US to find a record deal there. He found one with CBS. Early in 1976 we went to San Diego to play at the CBS convention. This took place at a big hotel, replete with ballrooms and swimming pools, which the company had taken over for their gathering and where they would banquet and watch performances by their current roster of artists. Our short performance took them by surprise – we weren't at all like the kind of mid-seventies acts they had been signing, not at all laid back or 'progressive'. We just rocked and rocked and did not let it go. After the show, the Big Boss Man came into our dressing room saying 'It'll be a sensation! A sensation!' He loved it, and so did CBS. Great things were expected of us and a US tour was arranged. CBS were making plans to launch us into the Big Time.

However, things weren't happy in the band. Lee and the others had begun drinking, while I, all my life a strict teetotaller, had acquired a heavy amphetamine habit. I liked speed because it could instantly banish the bouts of melancholy I had always been prone to. It makes you feel randy and enthusiastic, so you can spend all night and morning rolling around in bed, or writing songs, or putting all your albums in alphabetical order on the shelf. It also deprives you of sleep. I would stay up for three or four days at a time, sometimes more. After a debauch like this, your brain is scrambled – another thing that I enjoyed. I even liked the comedown, when it feels like Armageddon is looming just outside the window.

So there was I, a speed-freak with a puritanical attitude towards the alcohol that Lee was consuming, and strains began to show. A great antipathy grew between us. Why this was I don't know. We had been such friends in the early days and I had never ceased to admire Lee as a person and performer, but somehow we had begun to irritate each other.

Lemmy explained it by saying that speed-freaks and drunks just couldn't get along. At the time, Lemmy was living in squats and we spent a fair bit of time speeding and rapping through the night. I also became good friends with Mick Farren in Notting Hill. He had been one of the first *NME* journalists to champion Dr Feelgood and he was now writing his 'DNA Cowboys' trilogy of psychedelic science-fiction novels. I spent nights with him and his wife Ingrid listening to Bob Dylan and talking about William Burroughs. I loved Mickey – he had a good heart and all the idealism of the 1960s still lived within him. I'm really glad that I played on a couple of tracks on his weird and brilliant LP *Vampires Stole My Lunch Money*.

We did two tours of the USA in 1976, and CBS treated us like stars – we flew everywhere and stayed in good hotels, and we were interviewed by top rock papers and the *LA Times*. We played the Bottom Line in New York, supported by the Ramones, the Roxy in LA, and towns across America from Detroit to Dallas. The gigs were good and we took people by surprise with our full-on rock 'n' roll. We were making an impact everywhere we went.

But I wasn't happy. I had to write songs for the next album and this was proving difficult. Expectations were high and I had to come up with something to equal my previous successes. I was staying up for nights pacing round Holiday Inn rooms, speeding and trying to write new songs. My relationship with Lee was becoming more strained on the road. I was becoming isolated, up in my room, out of my mind, while the others were down in the bar talking about me. (Hotel walls are sometimes thin and I've lain on my bed on more than one occasion listening to tirades of drunken vituperation from the next room.)

This all led me to behave in a surly and unpleasant manner – in fact I became an arsehole. I wasn't happy. I wasn't talking. I was worrying about the album. I didn't like being away from home – I missed Irene and Matthew. And the more silent and miserable I became, the more they grew to dislike me, probably with good reason. I would sense their antipathy and fall into a silence, which irritated them more. All the time I'm thinking, 'I'm worried, I'm lonely. I don't want to upset everybody, but I feel so bad. Somebody help me.' But I didn't say nothin', and it just got worse and worse.

It got heavy – so heavy that Lee and I could hardly stand to be in the same room together. Mornings at airports and they would be at the bar drinking tequila, while I sat at a table feeling low and mean and wishing I was somewhere else instead. I checked in to the Holiday Inn in Hollywood (evading their 'no rock bands' policy with my pin-striped suit and briefcase) while everyone else was at the Hyatt House on Sunset Boulevard where the rock bands go.

I did not feel good. I drew the blinds so I didn't know if it was night or day, and walked around and around and I could not write any songs. When the time came to make our LA debut I walked down Sunset Boulevard to the Hyatt House and flopped on to my bed – I had been awake for two or three days. I slept.

The phone rang and they told me that Van Morrison was there and he wanted to meet me. Now, I am a Van Morrison fan – his lyrics and his phenomenal voice can really move me and have done since the days of Them. To me he was a hero. Special. And now I had to go and meet him in the state I was in.

We sat in the bar and talked. Van was nice as pie, very friendly, and he talked to me with complete modesty, as if he were no one special or as if I couldn't be expected to know who the hell he was. He said, 'I used to have a band a bit like yours, you know,' and I said, 'I know, I know.' I was in a kind of dream – it had happened so suddenly and here I was talking to the person who had made all that music that had moved me so much. We were in the bar of the Hyatt House, so I had to maintain my pose – Wilko Johnson, straight-faced, cool, talking to Van Morrison – but inside

I wanted to pour forth my gratitude and admiration in torrents of gushing praise.

As we shook hands when Van was leaving later that night I said, 'Thanks for *St Dominic's Preview*.' It scarcely did justice to my feelings for that album, but at least I said it.

When we got back to England we needed to make another album – I didn't have enough good material and we weren't sure what direction we should take – punk, inspired by ourselves in many ways, had erupted and changed everything. We decided to do the obvious thing and make a live album.

With Vic Maile again producing, we started listening to various concerts that had been recorded, and chose one from the Kursaal in Southend and one from Sheffield City Hall.

While we were doing this, Vic played some tracks just using the sound from the ambient microphones – that is, the 'audience' microphones. This gave an absolutely live sound – the sound that could be heard by the audience.

At that time if you bought a live album it was quite likely that most of the sound you heard was not in fact live, but had been overdubbed in a studio to improve the performance. Maybe you might hear just the bass drum beat from the original live show. When I heard the raw sound from these ambience microphones, I found it very exciting and I wanted to use the sound for our live album. Just as with our first album, I wanted to present Dr Feelgood straight, simple and as it really was.

Using the ambient sound in this way meant it was

impossible to overdub or replace any individual sound – you could mix the sounds from the close microphones on individual instruments into the overall sound, but you couldn't replace a part by overdubbing in the studio.

I wanted to use the ambient sound and told Vic Maile to produce the record like this. However, Andrew Lauder at the record company felt it was too crude and that the record should be produced in the conventional way, mixing the tracks without ambience and using overdubbing and studio production to tart up the live sound to make the record 'commercial'. There was a clash of opinions. Either the real live sound or a studio confection. Poor Vic Maile was caught in the middle, with me telling him to use the live sound and Andrew Lauder telling him to use studio production. I insisted on doing it my way and we carried on mixing the tracks like this, live without any overdubbing, against the opposition of the record company. Eventually Andrew Lauder backed down, telling Vic Maile to let me have my way and saying that the record would be a commercial failure, and I would have to do as I was told in future.

When we had finished mixing the album – to be entitled *Stupidity* – Chris came to me and said they would like to produce one of the tracks, 'Roxette', as a single, and they wanted to do this in the way Andrew Lauder had demanded. And they didn't want me in the studio when they did it. So I stayed at home while they went in and did a commercial, non-ambient production job on 'Roxette'. My way: their way. I was out on my own.

The album *Stupidity* went straight to No. 1 in the charts on release.

The production–job single 'Roxette' went nowhere.

So my intransigence had given Dr Feelgood their biggest ever record, but it had set me apart from the others.

The popularity of the album led to a highly successful UK tour, and differences were forgotten – for the time being.

CHAPTER 12

Dr Feelgood was getting bigger. Big. The Dr Feelgood logo
I had designed in the early days was now tattooed on arms,
drawn on schoolbooks, sold as badges everywhere.

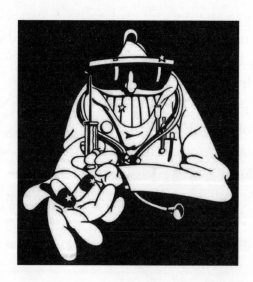

And there was money. Irene bought a house in a leafy suburb of Southend and we moved there with little Matthew. I doted on Matthew. Is there anything like the love you feel for a three-year-old child? That innocence and trust? You would fall down dead for them without a second thought.

Soon after we moved to our new house, Lee and Chris came knocking. They looked worried and said they had something to say. CBS in America, they told me, really wanted to do a job on our next album and push us up to playing stadiums, but to do so they wanted their own people to produce the record. I was still basking in the success of *Stupidity* and could do what I damned well pleased with regard to recording, and they knew my attitude to 'production', so they were worried.

I surprised them by saying I would be delighted to work with an American producer, so Lee and I went to the CBS convention in Atlanta to meet the man they had in mind – a charming black guy called Bert DeCouteaux who had worked with dozens of great musicians.

We were guests of honour at the convention and sat next to the boss of CBS in the banqueting hall. Once I was lost in the big hotel trying to find the main room to see Muddy Waters perform when a passing suit offered to show me the way. We walked along there not saying much, then as we entered the room, full of the CBS hierarchy, he flung his arm round my shoulder to show everyone what great mates we were. This sort of thing really does happen in the corporate world.

During the trip to Atlanta Lee and I were naturally forced into each other's company and we really made an effort to get along, I think successfully. We were even joking together like the old days and returned home in good spirits, ready to set about the album. Back in England, Lee started coming round my house of an afternoon with a bottle of vodka and spending time – we were trying to be friends again, I know we were.

We had a couple of gigs in newly post-Franco Spain, playing in big sports halls in Barcelona and Madrid. Our reputation had preceded us and the crowds were ecstatic. I remember getting a real kick seeing the Spanish crowd singing the lyrics to songs I had written in our bungalow back on Canvey Island. A big hall full of Spanish fans on our first trip to Spain and they knew all the songs. They were Dr Feelgood fans in a foreign land – our message was going out across the world, and it felt very good.

Back home from Spain, with the studio sessions approaching I took to lying on the floor downstairs at home all night with a tape recorder and a guitar, writing songs. The songs began to come and everything was rolling. Looking good.

The time came to go to Rockfield Studio near Monmouth. The studio is a converted farm with living accommodation. I went there with Irene and Matthew, feeling confident about the new songs I'd written. I was still writing when we got there – I even called in my great friend the poet Hugo Williams to help me. I had met Hugo in our early days playing in London – he had been following the band

and become fascinated by this bunch of yobbos, led by Lee Brilleaux, and wanted to write an article about us. When he approached us he was surprised to find that I was a poetry person and that I knew Tony Harrison. We sat in the van talking about poetry and rock 'n' roll and became lifelong friends.

The band fell into a routine of recording during the afternoon, then having dinner after which they would all go to the pub, and I would sit in my room writing lyrics. After they got back from the pub we would record into the night. The recording was being done in a more conventional multi-tracking manner than I liked, but I went along with Bert DeCouteaux's directions in the studio.

On the second or third day we tried out the song I had written called 'Sneaking Suspicion'. Bert DeCouteaux rushed out of the control room and said to me, 'Did you write that? It's a million-seller!' This from a guy who had worked on countless hit songs with stars like Stevie Wonder and Bobby Womack.

We set about recording it – I had imagined the song as being very raw and rough (I wanted it to sound like tug-boats and sirens and Canvey Island) but Bert DeCouteaux was giving it a polished, disco-like feel. For once, I didn't argue my case. After all, he could hear a million-seller in it.

At 2 a.m. we were listening to the playback. It did sound very commercial and everyone was very pleased with it. 'So this is what it all comes to,' I thought. 'I'm gonna be a millionaire. I'm gonna be rich and famous.' It was a melancholy feeling.

The next day, Lee came to see me and told me he felt

unable to sing one of the songs I had written with Hugo – it didn't feel right to him. Bert DeCouteaux told Lee to come to the studio with him and find a way round it, but I said, 'No – if he doesn't feel right with it, we'll abandon it.' Later, Chris took me to one side and started saying, 'You take these things too personally . . .' I realised he was talking about the abandoned song but I wondered what he meant . . .

Lew Lewis had written a song called 'Lucky Seven' and offered it to Lee for use on the album – they didn't want Lew to come to the studio with the song, so Lee had simply brought the lyrics, literally written on the back of a cigarette packet. One evening while I was sleeping, the band went into the studio and set these lyrics to a backing of their own devising – they recorded the whole thing without me, and somebody else playing the guitar. I was pleased to hear that the band had for the first time done some songwriting, but when I listened to it, it seemed to me that they had turned Lew's lyric into a rather mediocre pop song.

Another song was 'Paradise' – there were usually one or two songs that I would sing while Lee played harmonica or guitar in any album or live performance, and this was one of them. When I put the vocal on it, everybody heard the lyric for the first time; it was a song of love for Irene – the only time I ever used a real name in a song.

That night, after all the new songs had been put down, and Irene and Matthew had gone home, I was in my room writing lyrics. I was speeding of course, but it was really time for me to lie down and rest, when they all came back from the pub, tyres screeching. They came into my room – Figure wasn't with them – and sat down.

They had obviously been winding themselves up for something and they launched into a sneering denunciation of 'Paradise', calling it an ego trip and saying it was unsuitable for Dr Feelgood. I defended the song as I best could, but they pressed on with further criticisms of a more personal nature. They didn't like my dictatorial attitude to the music (the attitude I had adopted when we were making *Stupidity*). I felt this was unfair as I had been working under Bert DeCouteaux's direction without argument – yes, I had been dictatorial when making *Stupidity*, but *Stupidity* had been a huge success. Exasperated by their criticisms of 'Paradise', I told them I didn't like 'Lucky Seven', which they had made entirely without me. They chose to see this as another example of my egotism.

(For what it's worth, I'm still playing 'Paradise' forty years on – it's always been very popular with audiences; and Lew Lewis later recorded his own version of 'Lucky Seven' which was very different from the Feelgoods' effort, and which I never would have objected to – but they didn't want to listen to Lew and they didn't want to listen to me.)

The argument developed into a row about these two songs. They thought that I objected to 'Lucky Seven' because it was theirs and not mine. But there was more: they didn't like the way I lived my life, they didn't like the company I kept – they said they didn't like the silences I would fall into when I was depressed. They were taking it in turns to slag me off but, fuelled by amphetamine, I was easily able to rebuff their half-coherent criticisms. (At one point Lee shouted, 'Why is it that every time you say something it sounds fucking right?')

The whole thing escalated, as arguments will, until they were adamant that they wanted to use their rather feeble track, and I was telling them it wasn't a Dr Feelgood song, both stylistically and literally, since only half the band was playing on it with a keyboard player on the guitar. I told them they should give me the same consideration that I had given Lee over the Hugo Williams song – Lee didn't feel it was right, so we had abandoned it, and we should do the same with 'Lucky Seven' – that we all had always had an unspoken right of veto over anything we did and I was claiming that right now. Chris Fenwick misunderstood what I was saying and started talking about 'votes'.

I shouted, 'I said veto, not votes, you illiterate cunt!' and received such an evil look in reply that I knew I was out of the band.

It went on all night. By the morning I was out of Dr Feelgood. I say I was forced out. I didn't leave.

Looking back, I became convinced that they had planned the whole thing – they had tried to provoke an argument the day before, over Hugo's song, but I hadn't risen to it. They started the argument just as soon as my new songs were recorded – proof, as far as I was concerned, that they wanted my songs but they didn't want me. They conspired against me, used me and got rid of me. But I don't mind.

Later, we agreed that there would just be an announcement in the press to avoid any tedious bickering. We would work out a statement. No such thing happened. The front pages of all the music papers were covered with headlines saying I had left the band and stories explaining how it was all my fault, and how I had left the band after an argument about a Lew Lewis song. I didn't respond to this mendacious crap but stayed at home in a state of misery and confusion.

Then I went to see our accountant – he gave me some sagacious advice: 'It's crazy to break the band up now, when you're on the edge of something big. Swallow your pride, let them have their own way – if you're in the right that will become apparent – but right now, before things are irrevocable, go and make it up.' I knew he was speaking the truth and that was what I wanted to do. I walked down to Mortimer Street, to the record company.

Chris Fenwick came on the phone. I said, 'Listen, I'd like to have a meeting of the band so I can explain to everyone what I meant.' (Figure had not been present at the argument, and there had been people present who had no business there.) I wanted a meeting with just the five of us. I told Chris I would back down (from whatever it was) and let them have their way (in whatever it was) if it meant keeping the band together.

His tone was cold. It was that of someone who has made up their mind.

I said, 'Well, let's have a meeting.'

He said in a disinterested voice, 'You've got their numbers.'

I said, 'I don't think it's for me to call them up – I want a band meeting, just so I can explain to everyone.'

'Like I said, you've got their numbers.'

I said to him, 'Why don't you give yourself a treat and just say, *Fuck off, you cunt!*'

He said, 'Don't be like that.'

And that was the last parlay of Dr Feelgood.

—

CHAPTER 13

The bust-up of Dr Feelgood did nobody any good – certainly not me. I was left isolated, without a band or management of any kind, while they had the name and my songs. For every thousand people who had heard the name of Dr Feelgood, there were only a few who knew who Wilko Johnson was. I was destroyed.

They continued with hardly a moment's pause – playing a kind of boogie-lite on *Top of the Pops* and collaborating on songwriting and record production with pop singers. They blew away our image and began appearing dressed as characters from the geeky TV show *The Prisoner*. It was embarrassing. They went on until time and frequent personnel changes reduced them to a mediocre shadow of what we'd been in 1975. But they were still making a living with that name. Still performing my songs. Still using my logo.

WILKO JOHNSON

I had a flat in West Hampstead where I could stay when
I was in London. Jean-Jacques Burnel of the Stranglers
moved in and we became pretty good mates, and gradually
I began meeting the punk musicians who had sprung out of
nowhere in 1976 – The Clash, the Sex Pistols, The Damned.
The flat became a refuge for some of them and in the morning I would sometimes trip over Billy Idol or Rat Scabies.
One day I was walking along Oxford Street with my little
boy when three guys came running up. I recognised them
as The Clash, who were just beginning to make waves. Joe
Strummer said to me, 'You don't know who I am, but—'

I said, 'I know who you are, I've seen you in the papers.'

They were asking about the Dr Feelgood bust-up
and what I planned to do – I invited them over to West
Hampstead that afternoon. I arrived to find Lemmy hanging
out – I told him I'd met The Clash and had invited them
over.

Lemmy snarled, 'The Clash! Did you see what their
roadie said about our last single?'

I was treated to the rather pleasing image of The Clash
and Motörhead fighting on my living-room floor. But the
afternoon passed convivially.

I was a star now, but Lemmy had been sacked by
Hawkwind and was living in penury while he put his new
band Motörhead together. I used to go round there and
turn them on – I enjoyed being rich and being able to treat
my friends; like the silk merchant in Varanasi said, 'Money
is like water.' Lemmy was good company, intelligent and
witty, and he had a kind of twisted wisdom. As fellow
speed-freaks (Mick Farren reckoned I was the only bloke

who was able to keep up with Lemmy), we often spent whole nights rapping.

But once we nearly came to blows. It was in the Virgin Records office. There was trouble over a woman and I was shouting, 'You've got too much fucking lip!'

Some New Wave musicians happened to be there, and they all took cover.

I grabbed Lemmy's jacket, but Lemmy just stood there glaring in my eyes and shouting, 'Go on! Nut me! Nut me!' Of course I couldn't do that, so I started headbutting the wall. All this was taking place in a passageway and Richard Branson and his people were having to squeeze past us as we argued. We ended up slobbering on each other's shoulders and cursing all trifling women.

A lot of crazy things happened in that flat, but it really is a blur of sex and drug excess. I still get a nostalgic kick if I ever pass by it.

Once a bunch of us planned a weekend at Beverley Martyn's house in Sussex (Beverley's been a good friend since she knocked me off my feet with her great voice and songs in 1978). In the evening I was to travel down by train with John Lydon. I met him at Victoria and we set off. Some teenage boys walked in the corridor past our first-class compartment and did a double-take when they saw us. They came into the compartment and talked with us for a while – a great story for their friends at school on Monday.

Our train soon stopped, stranding us at Tonbridge station. It was late evening and the station was full of people coming out of the pubs and discos. John was still regarded as a monster in the tabloids, and we sat there trying to hide from *hoi polloi* as freight trains went banging past.

We finally arrived in Sussex, only to find the little local station deserted and fogbound. There were footsteps approaching and out of the fog loomed a policeman. We told him we had been expecting a car to meet us and we needed to make a phone call. He led us to the other side of the station where there was a phone box. As we crossed the bridge he kept looking at John, obviously recognising a felon who should be arrested.

'What did you say your name was?'

'John Lydon.'

'Hmm.'

We got to the telephone. The number we needed was in my briefcase.

I had a gun in the briefcase – a Walther LP53, the same gun that Sean Connery holds in the famous picture of James Bond. In fact it's an air pistol (yes, the gun that Sean Connery poses with is a Walther LP53 air pistol), but it looks pretty lethal and I really didn't want the cop to see it. He thought we were up to no good and he wasn't going to leave us alone. I stood in front of the telephone dithering with the clasps of my briefcase. An eternity passed before our friends' car emerged from the fog.

We had a good weekend, though I don't know what we were doing – talking and shooting the air pistol probably.

I was very confused during those days, miserable and keeping my spirits up with amphetamine, and I started to discover things about people that you don't learn in school. When I wanted to form a band of my own I turned to some good old friends from the pub rock days. If you're rich and famous it's amazing how many friends you get. Very good friends.

Eventually I fell in with what I thought would be a good band, who came to me out of nowhere. Though they were all quite unknown, I arranged the band on a basis of equality – money, everything. I thought this would mean that everybody would be totally committed to the band. Wrong. They all thought they were stars, and I was just a stepping stone to the Big Time for them. We went into a studio with Vic Maile to make some demos for the record company and during a break in the recording Vic told me that these people were wrong. I didn't want to listen. He told me that I should wait until the right people could be found – that I could take a year off if necessary. I wouldn't believe him – I thought that I must get straight back on the road or I would be forgotten. But Vic had seen through these people and their attitude towards me and he was telling me the truth. They really weren't into my music – and they had aspirations of their own.

I went into the record company with the demos we had made, and they called me into the MD's office. They told me that they were ending my contract – I no longer had a record deal. And they told me that Dr Feelgood, now their biggest act, were insisting on this. If they were trying to ruin my career they should have just left that to me.

I wanted to be in a band, not a solo performer, so I called the band Solid Senders, not Wilko Johnson – all equal. I told promoters not to bill my name, just Solid Senders, and I thought we'd earn our own reputation on the road.

It used to infuriate me to see 'ex-Dr Feelgood' on gig posters. (Really Dr Feelgood should have billed themselves as 'ex-Wilko Johnson'.)

I can't believe I was so stupid, but I made myself believe in that band. They were OK as musicians and our live gigs went very well, but they weren't mates – there was none of that solidarity and belief that makes you feel strong enough to take on the world.

All this time I was besieged by offers from record companies – I was hot property.

Eventually we signed with Virgin. There was a lot of money involved (these were the days of big advances) and the band were very eager to spend it. We chose to record our first album at the hugely expensive Manor studio, which belonged to Virgin. It is actually a big manor house in its own grounds and you can spend all day rolling in the four-poster beds or lingering over the cordon-bleu cooking. Irish wolfhounds lie in front of the fire.

This – by far the most expensive album I had ever made – was also taking a lot of time and I was beginning to see what Vic Maile had told me – these weren't the people for me. It just wasn't a band. Whereas Dr Feelgood had started in friendship and love of the music, this was just an exercise in ambition.

I was out of my head all the time – the producer had to come and tell me that the others were wasting our time by hassling him. They wanted him to record their compositions or they wanted to spend hours perfecting their own parts. I had to tell them off and remind them we were supposed to be a band, not a collection of opportunists.

But there was never that feeling of belief in what you were doing, and belief in each other that had been the foundation of Dr Feelgood. I had a bad feeling about this album. It was no fun.

On the very last night of recording, we had one more track to do to complete the album. Richard Branson and his people were there watching proceedings. The keyboard player chose this moment to throw a wobbler and walk out of the band. Pretty embarrassing.

We finished the album in London, with a version of 'Shop Around'. I got my old friend John Denton to play the piano. He'd never been in a recording studio before, but JD really rocks – he couldn't keep the headphones on, he was rocking so much. He is also a brilliant, if eccentric, pianist and I wanted him in the band, with his wild piano and his wilder stage show. But JD had a good job – he was a senior VAT inspector – and he refused to go professional, no matter what I offered him. (What a rocking VAT man!) It was a shame about JD. I loved his piano playing, which was very distinctive, very spiky, and I loved his uninhibited stage manner and the way we could communicate on stage. He was the first musician I had really interacted with since Lee Brilleaux. He loved to play, and with his stage image – that of a kind of deranged, leather-jacketed rocker – he could have been a contender. It always worked perfectly between us and we played a lot of gigs together. But he wouldn't go professional.

The album *Solid Senders* was released to fair reviews and poor sales. We toured the UK and Europe. You know when things ain't right, they all go wrong, Virgin lost interest and the contract was terminated.

117

I then got a very keen offer from Polydor, and we went into their studio to make a couple of demos. That day, though, JD told me he felt bad vibes.

The following day, Alan Black, the Polydor A&R man, phoned and told me he wanted to give me some advice – get rid of the band. They weren't on my side, in fact they were actively hostile to me. During the recording session they had been coming up to him when my back was turned and urging him to listen to some demos of songs they'd written, more or less dismissing my stuff as worthless. Alan said he was very keen to sign me, but not with the band – he did not want anything to do with them. 'They' were the bass player and drummer – JD of course (an actual friend; a geezer from Southend who I had been at school with) was not part of this betrayal.

I had risked my reputation (and a lot of my money) to try and create a real band of equals, striving together for success, and had ended up with a situation Lucrezia Borgia would have been at home in. Vic Maile had told me from the outset and Alan Black at the end – it wasn't the right band for me.

I had blown it. My fifteen minutes was over. I recruited a local bass player and drummer – Russell Strothard and Alex Bines – and set off on the road. Irene looked after the telephone. My reputation was still sufficient to draw audiences all round the UK and Europe, and we had plenty of work and some pretty good times.

With French Henri in his Volkswagen minibus we must have travelled thousands of miles through France, Spain and Scandinavia, as well as the UK. (French Henri is a well-known Southend character – for many years he ran the *Golden Hind*, a replica of Drake's ship that stood by Southend pier. There were waxworks on this ship, including, rather anachronistically, The Beatles; one time I arrived home on the eve of my birthday to find a present from Henri in the shape of a cardboard box. I put my hand into this box, felt some hair, and withdrew the wax head of Paul McCartney. It was pretty freaky – Irene found it so disturbing that it was banished to the garage for a long time before being allowed back into the house to sit on top of the piano. Now only a glass eye remains.)

For a while I had a band with Lew Lewis. I had known him for a long time and really liked his harmonica playing and curious songs, but I knew he was genuinely wild. I flattered myself I could keep him in order, but it was chaotic. We went on stage once and started our set with 'Shake And Finger Pop', but Lew sang a completely different song – 'Messing With The Kid' – all the way through, and never realised. When he was together Lew could be brilliant, even inspired, and I hoped to forge a partnership with him like I'd had with Lee Brilleaux, but Lew wasn't always together – and neither was I.

To play the drums we got in Topper Headon, who had recently been ejected from The Clash as a result of his drug problems – I thought it might be funny to watch Lew and Topper trying to borrow a fiver off each other. We played about five gigs, including the Marquee and the Reading Festival, and they were good gigs. Something might have come of that band, but it wasn't to be. I have an abiding image in my mind of turning round on stage at the Marquee to see Topper leaning over his drums and projectile vomiting without missing a beat. He told me that it often happened. That's punk, I suppose.

The band with Lew finished with a long and disastrous tour of Europe and Scandinavia. It bankrupted me. I ended up paying the debts and they all buggered off and left me. I scraped another band together, but eventually things began to slow down and gigs got scarcer. It looked like time to quit.

CHAPTER 14

Just then I ran into Ian Dury and Davey Payne at a show. I had known them since the pub days when they were in Kilburn & the High Roads, but now, of course, they had achieved great success as Ian Dury and the Blockheads with songs like 'Hit Me With Your Rhythm Stick' and 'Reasons To Be Cheerful'. Davey, the saxophonist, is a wiry guy with drilling eyes. He radiates danger. I really liked Davey and I started telling him my troubles – how I thought I was going to quit. The next day I saw Ian again and he told me that the Blockheads were in the studio and would I like to come down and make a record with them. Ian had an idea to record me singing 'Lonesome Me', because he thought I looked lonely out on stage.

Naturally I jumped at the chance. Not only were the Blockheads one of the best bands around musically, but they had among their number the phenomenal bass player

Norman Watt-Roy, who had created the celebrated bass line to 'Hit Me With Your Rhythm Stick', and gave the Blockheads their unrivalled funk.

I found the Blockheads down in a little studio in Knightsbridge. Ian and Davey I already knew. Then there was Johnny Turnbull the lead guitarist, a very perky Geordie, and Mickey Gallagher, a rather more solemn Geordie, on keyboards. Norman Watt-Roy was an Anglo-Indian who seemed to live for playing the bass, getting stoned and laughing, and on the drum kit was Charlie Charles, a black guy with a thousand-watt smile. Charlie was a great drummer and could hit the drums louder than anyone I've ever heard, and he could light a room up with his presence. His power and funky feel worked with Norman's bass lines to make up one of the best rhythm sections anywhere. My own style of playing is based around rhythm. I'm a rhythm guitarist, so I could jump right in with these two. We recorded a reggae-slanted version of 'Lonesome Me' which I think was pretty good. It came out as a single on the Blockhead label (part of Stiff Records), and sold not at all.

Ian nevertheless asked me to join the Blockheads. They needed someone to replace his writing partner and keyboard player/guitarist Chaz Jankel, who had left the band, and they had been off the road for some time in the process of making their next album. Ian had allowed several months to do this – I had never spent more than three or four weeks recording an album. A season ticket got me commuting between Southend and Knightsbridge three or four days a week.

I realised the Blockheads were a bit stumped – Chaz

Canvey Island flood, 1953. *(Photo credit: PA)*

Shell Haven Refinery. *(Photo credit: David Burke)*

Irene's Telecaster.

(Photo credit: Malcolm Wilkinson)

Wedding. *(Photo credit: Big Figure)*

Afghan shirt.
(Photo credit: Fred Ligterink)

Dr Feelgood, 1975.
(Photo credit: Keith Morris)

Breakdown.
(Photo credit: Hugo Williams)

Ian Dury and the Blockheads.
(Photo credit: Francis Newman)

'You c★★t!'
(Photo credit: Wilko Johnson)

Domestic bliss. *(Photo credit: Wilko Johnson)*

Irene, Simon, Wilko, Laura, Keiko, Yuriko. Painting by Malcolm Wilkinson.

(Photo credit: John Palmer)

Taku Taku. *(Photo credit: Hiroki Nishioka)*

Fuji Rock, 2013. *(Photo credit: Hiroki Nishioka)*

With Hugo Williams.
(Photo credit: Murphy Williams)

Brothers. *(Photo credit: Malcolm Wilkinson)*

Railway Hotel with
Mike and French Henri.
(Photo credit: Mickey Fawcett)

Wilko Johnson Band.
(Photo credit: Simon Reed)

Roger Daltrey and guitarist.
(Photo credit: Mickey Fawcett)

With Charlie Chan
and Mr Huguet.
(Photo credit: Charlie Chan)

Jankel had been their musical director, as well as a song-writer and musician, and in his absence they were trying to produce the album themselves. I also saw that the guys in the band were by no means well off when you considered the massive record sales they had generated. Discontent and old resentments were simmering and would sometimes erupt as we spent days and weeks in that little studio. Ian would mollify people with promises of bigger money for this album.

Ian, who wrote his brilliant lyrics without music, was collaborating with members of the band to write the songs. I wrote a couple. The recording was shambolic without a producer in charge, and stumbled on until it even broke the generous deadline it had been given. Still we got the album, *Laughter*, ready for our tour of the UK in December.

Ian was still enormously popular and we played to big partisan audiences and full houses. They loved Ian. I really enjoyed being part of that killer rhythm section, leaving all the front-man, stage-fright stuff to Ian. He was a great front man. Even among a collection of very watchable performers like the Blockheads, he dominated the stage with his presence, his single Gene Vincent glove and his novelty props. He was sinister and amusing. His dodgy, rough voice was the perfect vehicle for his poetic and insightful songs.

Ian had a kind, if complicated, heart and was usually good and entertaining company, but he had a very dark side which could emerge after one drink too many – which was usually one. He had had a traumatic childhood, being crippled at an early age by polio and suffering at a succession of boarding

123

schools. He once told me that he had grown accustomed, when he was a child, to people staring at him because he was a cripple, and now that he was famous and people looked at him for that reason, he still felt pangs of the old hurt.

But he could be a devil. Once we were in a posh hotel in Copenhagen waiting to play the big Pinkpop festival. The hotel was full of bands from all over the world as well as the usual well-heeled clientele and I was in my room relaxing. The phone rang. It was the tour manager asking me to go down to the bar where Ian was causing trouble. Ian used to play a game where he would offend and upset somebody and then try to win them over with his charm. I think he did it because he could never quite believe that anybody could like or love him, and he wanted to test them. He would play this game on total strangers sometimes, and pitch it very strong, and I do believe he could be the most offensive person I have ever encountered.

Down in the bar, Ian was face to face with an American guy. He was leaning into him, telling him that he could make him like him just with words. The guy was furious and on the point of thumping Ian, but Ian wouldn't back off. I got in between them and made profuse apologies to the American. When I turned around Ian was sitting at the bar with Norman and Raymond, his jovial Rasta minder, trying to persuade him to go to bed.

Ian grew louder and more obstreperous. He was annoying everybody in the bar, so we seized him and manhandled him off the bar stool. He grabbed hold of the brass bar rail and began shouting, 'Help! Help me!' and a tug-of-war developed. We dragged him out of the bar and into the foyer, where people entering the hotel were treated to the sight of two spivs and a big Rasta dragging a cripple into the lift while he cried out for help. In Ian's room we threw him on the bed and took the calliper off his leg. Ian couldn't walk without it, and this was a recognised method of immobilising him. We left him there shouting, 'You bastards! You're all fucking sacked!'

It wasn't only Ian who caused trouble. One time we were touring Australia. Ian was hugely popular and we were playing big gigs. The Blockheads (and Ian) were on top form. It was such a kick when the stage lights went up and we went into 'Sex And Drugs And Rock 'n' Roll'. What they call a tumultuous reception. I was really enjoying the tour.

Somewhere along the way we picked up this character called Spartacus, who played bass for the African band Osibisa. Spartacus started getting up on stage with us – he would stand beside me and we would do that running-on-the-spot reggae thing. One night in Canberra we were doing this when suddenly the sound collapsed into chaos and the drums stopped. Davey, Johnny and Charlie were fighting on the stage. Spartacus and I looked at each other, shrugged and carried on running on the spot. What had happened was this – Davey, always ready for a lark, had squirted a container of talcum powder into one of the stage fans, and the resulting cloud had covered Johnny, who is very particular about his clothes. A scuffle ensued. Seeing this, Charlie had vaulted over his drum kit and joined the mêlée. The audience loved it as the fight went on and the rest of us continued playing. Order was eventually restored with help from the roadies and we finished the gig in fine style. One of the guys from the Australian support band said to me, 'D'you do that every night?'

Ian also got us all banned for life from the Sebel Townhouse hotel in Sydney. But that's another story. I didn't witness that particular outrage, but it was outrageous.

Here's a story I *can* tell, though. We'd played a great gig in Dublin, and everyone was invited to Ian's suite back at the hotel. When I got there, there was a party going on with a room full of people from the gig. Although I was strictly teetotal at that time, I took a glass of champagne and started talking to some girls. Suddenly Davey Payne rushed into the room, came up to me and said, 'Wilko, I've just knocked Ian out.'

We went out on to the balcony and he told me what had happened: Ian and Davey had been arguing in the corridor (there was always an intense and lingering hatred between the two of them), and Davey had grabbed Ian by the lapels and swung him round. Ian had lost his balance, fallen and banged his head on the wall.

We returned to the room in time to see big Raymond coming through the door holding Ian in his arms like a broken ventriloquist's dummy. His shades were crooked across his face. The party was over – the guests were ejected and the band was summoned to Ian's room for a conference.

I walked in there still tipsy from the unaccustomed alcohol to find Ian sitting on the bed and the band gathered round the room.

Ian said, 'Do you know what he did to me? Feel that!'

He grabbed my wrist and forced my hand on to his head where there was indeed a considerable bump.

He said, 'This meeting is to decide whether to quit the tour now, or go on without Davey Payne.' He was proposing to sack one of the Blockheads' main attractions, and I stepped forward half drunk and said, 'I've already seen one great band break up over nothing and I'm fucked if I'm gonna see another.' We were batting this back and forth when Davey suddenly rushed violently towards Ian, who fell back on the bed and cried out in terror. Davey stopped in the middle of the room, pointed at Ian and burst into malicious laughter.

In the end it was decided to fine Davey £200 and carry on. The road crew had a blackboard and were chalking up odds as to who would be the next to hit Ian. The favourite was often Ian Dury.

I really enjoyed working with the Blockheads, but Ian would take long periods off the road, so I took to playing clubs with my own band. Back in the clubs and small gigs after the big tours with the Blockheads, I managed to scrape a living until things began running down and it looked like quitting time again. In 1984 I had five more gigs left.

I needed a bass player, so I called Norman, who I hadn't seen in quite a while.

I said, 'Can you do five gigs with me?' and Norman, who wasn't doing much himself, said, 'Yes.'

So there was me, Norman and Sav (Salvatore Ramundo, my Italian drummer, who talked just like an Essex boy but didn't know a word of English before he was twelve). We did the five gigs and just carried on, starting to get plenty of work in clubs and smaller venues. Norman had a following of his own who would gather at his side of the stage to watch him do his stuff. We would pack the Half Moon in Putney, the Powerhouse in Islington and the Mean Fiddler, and gigs up and down the country. Just the three of us and Robbie the roadie in our Transit van. Sav would drive and the rest of us would get stoned. We were pretty happy – we always got on well together – and we were earning regular money.

Just after we started the band in February 1985, Irene told me she was pregnant, twelve years after Matthew had been born. (I remember nine months later running to the hospital with Matthew to meet baby brother Simon.)

Then Mr Masahiro 'Masa' Hidaka came to see us playing at the 100 Club. He told us that he was the head of Smash Corporation, a Japanese promotion company, and offered us a tour of Japan. Well, yes, we said – none of us had ever been there and the money was very good – this was at the time of the Japanese 'bubble' economy.

I fell in love with Japan straight away – from the dazzling, neon-blasted streets of Tokyo, to the beautiful pagodas and temples of Kyoto and Nara, to the people themselves, who understand jokes. And seafood, and chopsticks.

They treated us like stars. There were even teenage girls screaming as we got out of the car. After the gigs they would form long orderly queues as we sat at tables signing autographs. Many of them would be literally shaking with nerves and bowing compulsively on meeting us. You couldn't help but be charmed.

The gigs went really well and we went back the next year. And the next, and so on. Japan became the high point of our year – a place where it was groovy to be, and where we were stars. One time when we did our annual tour of Japan, we found that Dr Feelgood were our support band on a couple of gigs. Believe me, they were feeble – it was sad to see them. We didn't talk.

I hadn't been in contact with Lee Brilleaux or the other Feelgoods since our break-up in 1977 – just a couple of chance meetings where people looked at their shoes and said, 'How're you going?' Then I heard that Lee had terminal cancer. I didn't know what to do – it had been nearly twenty years since we had seen each other and I didn't know if he would want to see me. I couldn't just go there – I would need to be invited. But my brother Malcolm went to see Lee and came and told me that he thought he would like me to visit. I said I would need some of the Feelgoods' people to take me there (I didn't even know where to go). While we were waiting for this to be arranged, Lee died. (On the same day as Kurt Cobain.)

After Lee's funeral, everybody went down to the Dr Feelgood bar on Canvey Island. There was a party going on and people were playing music. Somebody put a guitar in my hand and I got up on stage. And there we were – me, Sparko and Figure, putting our guitars on and getting behind the drums. We played 'She Does It Right' with that empty space in the middle of the stage. It was unbearably poignant. I came off stage to find Irene crying on Chris's shoulder and everybody overcome. All looking back on those magic times so long ago. Figure and Sparko and I had looked at each other and said, 'What did we do?' Yeah. What did we do?

*

We made many friends in Japan – Masa and his people at Smash Corporation, and musicians like Sheena & the Rokkets and Thee Michelle Gun Elephant. There were also fans. Keiko Shimizu and Yuriko Daikoku were two girls among a group of fans who used to come to every gig we played in Japan. Eventually they came to England, visited our house and became great friends of our family. Sometimes they came with other Japanese friends for Christmas – little Simon must have thought that Christmas was a time when the house filled up with Japanese ladies who taught him to count and say rude words in Japanese.

And so it went on – me, Sav and Norman in our customised Transit van with aircraft seats and a good stereo, gigging in clubs in London and round the UK, and tours of Spain, France, Scandinavia and Japan. We made a couple of albums which we released on independent record labels in the various territories where we worked. Irene looked after the business from a tiny office at the end of the kitchen. I suppose we had a little rock 'n' roll cottage industry. We moved round the corner to a smaller (but groovier) house. Matt had his own place, and Simon was a teenager.

That was a happy home. Me, Simon and Irene, and Matthew living nearby.

Then in early 2004, Irene began to lose weight dramatically, and her usual vitality and energy were draining away. Tests discovered an advanced and inoperable bowel cancer. She was going to die.

CHAPTER 15

We cancelled all our gigs so I could be at home with Irene. Oh, those days. She made us keep her illness secret, apart from close friends, because she didn't want her mother, who was suffering from dementia, to worry. Her friend Sue used to take her over to Canvey Island every Friday to do the housekeeping for her mum – Ivy never noticed as Irene grew weaker, she would just sit while Sue did the chores. She bore her illness with serene patience. All her concern was with the welfare of others – her mother, and our sons Matthew and Simon. She never once complained.

I would see her digging in the garden, planting flowers she would never see in bloom, or sitting on the stairs rocking gently back and forth and singing to herself.

Her birthday came. I had been making animations on my computer – the kind of trippy scenes I had once wanted to paint, only these scenes were animated. It was painstaking work, and I often sat up all night working frame by frame through long sequences to produce quite small changes.

That morning I was working on one of my favourites, a scene showing the medieval poet William Langland and his vision of Piers Plowman on the Malvern Hills. The poet sat by a stream in a green landscape, looking up and sometimes lifting his hand to a tower full of stone faces which constantly changed their expressions and flowed into different shapes and patterns. There was a deep dungeon below and in the middle distance, the Field Full of Folk; processions of people marching in slow circles. The sky was full of ranks of cloud-angels making slow synchronised gestures.

I had created several of these animated scenes, which had gradually evolved over months and years (most were subsequently lost in a hard-drive disaster – always double back up your work!).

I was pretty pleased with my night's efforts; Irene came and looked at it and said, 'Has that changed at all in the last three years?' Completely without sarcasm or malice, she was simply expressing a friendly interest, but had gone right to the truth of the matter – despite all the hours and nights I had spent, it really hadn't changed much.

All the love I had for her sweet and unspoiled nature welled up in me and I said, 'Oh how can I ever live without you?' I made her a birthday card from a still of the animation, saying '*You* never changed'.

The days passed. Drinking. Stupefied by downers, high on amphetamine, I was losing her and nothing could be done. I would sit downstairs thinking, 'She's upstairs. Now.

But time is taking her away with every moment that passes. If only we could remain here.'

> *But here upon this bank and shoal of time*
> *We'd jump the life to come.*

Go upstairs to see her, but what to do, what to say? Sitting by her bedside talking about the word 'crepuscular' as the sunset faded outside the window. Watching her sleep, hoping that she was in some beautiful dream far away from pain and sorrow.

The summer came. Four months had passed since the diagnosis, and Irene was growing very weak and tired as the life drained from her. We decided that she should spend a few days at my brother's place in Salisbury, where Malcolm and Laura could provide tranquillity and good cooking – two things I'm not very good at. As she walked out to the car she was unsteady on her feet. The car drove off and I went back indoors to take drugs.

After a few days Malcolm called to tell me that Irene was feeling very unwell and wanted to come home.

Oh God, here it comes. I felt numb and helpless. Malcolm called again to say that Irene had been taken into hospital, and I set off with Matthew as night was falling to drive to Salisbury. The hospital allowed us to come in at that late hour for a brief visit and we stood round her bed – me and Matthew and Malcolm and Laura.

She looked so thin and frail, but there, weary from suffering, was her beautiful smile. She was too tired to talk – anyway, what was there to say? I did a little dance for her at the end of the bed and then we waved and walked out into the night. My emotions were in turmoil – I wanted to cry out and roar in my pain and helplessness, but I couldn't make a disturbance outside the hospital so I just shook my fist at the stars. This self-conscious theatrical gesture felt feeble and embarrassing. Fortunately, the stars took no notice.

The next day we sat in a small room with a doctor. I said, 'She's dying, isn't she?' and the doctor said yes, her instinct told her that it would not be today or tomorrow, but very soon. They could either try and build up her strength enough to travel home or take her into the hospice.

The hospice is a quiet place at the far end of the long, sprawling hospital – there is a garden with a pond and fields all around. The people there treated Irene with such deep and genuinely loving care – she could not have been in better hands. They did all the things that I would have been hopelessly incompetent at, like turning her over in bed, and they did them not only with the skill of long practice but with a never-failing affection in their soothing words. I can't express the gratitude I felt for them. They took away the IV tubes and stuff – her body could no longer absorb nutrients and the tubes were just a source of discomfort. And so she lay in bed, sunlight slanting through that quiet room, her voice reduced to a whisper. I would sit all night by her bed-side, starting out of sleep to see if she still breathed.

Days went by. In the garden outside the room where she lay sleeping – Matthew and Simon sat together under the trees, and I wondered what they were feeling – we were cut off like lifeboats scattering around some tragic wreck. I would go into Salisbury Cathedral and find some solace

in that beautiful place, becoming one with the untold generations who had gone before, whose feet had trod those
flagstones and whose eyes had lifted in wonder to that soar-
ing vault above.

One evening I got a bottle of whisky and became very
drunk. I ran from the hospice and found myself in the
gathering twilight at a bus shelter on the edge of Salisbury
Plain. Matthew and Simon came out to find me. I launched
into a grandiose speech about life, the universe and
everything. Drunk. Drunk. They went back to the hospice
and I walked off in the direction of Salisbury, still drinking
from my bottle of whisky.

It was late now, and dark. A bunch of teenage boys were
playing football in the street and I sat down on a garden
wall to watch when my phone rang. It was Matthew, asking
where I was so he could come and get me. For some reason
I replied, 'I'm in Warminster.' One of the boys stopped
playing football and said to me, 'You ain't in Warminster,
you're in Salisbury.'

I stood up and said, 'My wife, you know, she's dying –
she's down at the hospital dying of cancer. We've been
together for forty years and now she's dying and there's
nothing that can help.'

The boys stopped kicking the ball and gathered round
to hear my sad story. I spoke about time and mortality. I
said, 'You guys are young – you've got eternity in front of
you, it's great, it's great – but my whole world is coming
to an end. My old lady, she's dying, she's really dying.' I
told them I had once been famous long before they were
born, and that it was a really good career choice, and

asked if any of them played music. Some of them said they did, and I said, 'Yeah, go for it – it's really good fun and you can make a million dollars and get all the girls.' I walked away from them still drinking from my bottle.

In the dead waste and middle of the night, I came walking along the greensward by the river where rain had made the ground very muddy. The whisky was all gone and I was hopelessly, staggering drunk. I fell, sprawling face down in the mud. It was that kind of drunkenness where you know you can't possibly move for at least half an hour. I got out my mobile phone to call Matthew. The battery was dead. So there I lay in the mud, unable to call for help or tell anyone where I was. Pretty wretched.

The sky was growing light with dawn by the time I was able to get to my feet. I was covered in mud. I decided to go home to Southend to get cleaned up and caught an early train. At home I found I had lost my key and I had to kick the door in to gain access.

I was just about ready to go back to Salisbury when the phone rang. It was Matthew telling me that Irene had died. Oh.

The hospice said that if I came immediately I would be able to see her. I called a friend who had a car and we set off for Salisbury, driving through that blazing August day without a word. I was thinking, 'What am I gonna see? What am I going to feel?' The universe was dissolving.

We arrived at the hospice and waited for Matthew and Simon, then a nurse came and led us across to the mortuary. Big door opens. 'She's in there.'

She was lying on a table wearing a long robe. With her

hollow face, lips slightly parted, she looked like a saint on a medieval tomb.

I walked up to her, raised my arms and felt – I don't know what – numb disbelief. I never expected to see this . . . John Denton had once remarked that if he were dying he would like Irene to be at his bedside. This was such an apt tribute to her nature that I always pictured it for myself. She would be with me to the end.

Now I was looking down on her poor corpse. She had gone. My one sure thing in the universe was gone.

I whispered in her ear and kissed her lips. They were cold. I remembered that first kiss at her gate more than forty years before. Gone, gone.

That night, Matthew and Simon and I went drinking all round Salisbury. In the morning, among the concerns about death certificates and so on, I realised that I would have to tell Irene's mother. She didn't even know that Irene was sick, and now I would have to tell her that her only child was dead.

I called Sue, who had been caring for Ivy all through Irene's sickness. Sue and Irene had been such close friends they were like sisters. She told me to call the Reverend Brenda. Of course. The Reverend Brenda was the minister at the Canvey Island Methodist Church to which Ivy belonged. I had met her four years before, when I had been impressed by her dignified conduct of Irene's father's funeral. I called her and told her what had happened. She, like most people, knew nothing of Irene's illness, so quiet had we kept it to avoid worrying Ivy.

We met near Ivy's house. We walked along the street and

through that gate where a kiss had changed my life. I could feel my heart breaking; an immense weight seemed to be pressing down on my spirit.

Ivy opened the back door. She was delighted to see us and began greeting us effusively. It didn't occur to her how strange a sight it was to see me in the company of the vicar.

The Reverend Brenda calmed her down and sat with her, and began telling her that Irene had been very ill. 'Oh, I didn't know.'

'No, she didn't want to worry you.'

I was sitting on the other side of the room, numb with grief as this small tragedy – one domestic scene among millions around the world at that moment, but to me the very crux and archetype of death and sorrow – was enacted.

Then the Reverend Brenda very gently told Ivy that her beloved daughter was dead.

Ivy cried, 'Oh no!' in her Glaswegian accent.

It was the saddest sound I ever heard.

CHAPTER 16

Irene had always wanted a green funeral. We found a place
up in Essex where they are creating a woodland by planting
a tree over every grave. Simple wooden plaques which will
eventually decay into the earth show the names of the dead.
I bought two slots side by side.

The day came for the funeral. While the Reverend Brenda
held a service for Ivy and her friends at the Canvey Island
Methodist Church, we gathered at the burial ground near
Wrabness – friends, people from the biz, from Dr Feelgood
and the Blockheads, people from Japan (Keiko Shimizu,
who could not be there, later flew from Tokyo for just two
days in order to say her prayers at the graveside. Irene had
always felt a deep affection for Keiko). They brought Irene
from Salisbury in a green van. We carried the simple coffin
across the field to the graveside and listened to the sublime
voice of Lata Mangeshkar singing 'Tu Kitni Achchi Hai – O

Ma', a heartbreaking Bollywood song that means 'You are so good – oh, Mother'. The words just summed up Irene.

> *This world is a jungle of thorns*
> *You are the flower garden. Oh, Mother*

Looking at that wooden box, listening to that song, thinking of all the years. I made a short speech and managed to keep my composure, then

> *Lay her in the earth*
> *And from her fair and unpolluted flesh*
> *May violets spring*

As they lowered her down to the sound of Leadbelly singing 'Irene Goodnight', I broke down.

> *I love Irene, God knows I do,*
> *Love her till the sea runs dry,*
> *If Irene turn her back on me*
> *I'm gonna take morphine and die*
> *Irene goodnight . . .*

Racked with sobbing, I stood in a dream where people scattered earth into the grave of the only one I ever loved. I walked away from the graveside and across the field on my own. As I stepped into the lane, suddenly sheltered from the wind, I realised I was walking on another planet in an impossible universe where she did not exist.

CHAPTER 17

'I want her back.' I could not speak or even think these words without breaking down. I would break down in tears in the street and have to find some corner to hide. A song on the radio would hit me like a blow. I walked through crowded places feeling like a ghost in an unreal world, lost to everything but my sorrow. I thought of her every waking moment and of course she haunted my dreams – sometimes those lucid dreams where you know you are dreaming; then I could really be with her and hold her in my arms for precious moments before

I waked, she fled and day brought back my night.

Waking in the morning thinking something's wrong – 'What is it that's wrong?' – and then remembering. The sadness of everyday things; memories of youth, regret for every moment spent away from home doing rock 'n' roll; regret for every day I did not fall down at her feet and say, 'I love you.'

> Quit rambling and quit gambling
> Quit staying out late at night
> Go home to your wife and your family
> And sit down by the fireside bright
> Irene goodnight . . .

Sue continued to care for Ivy, and I would go over to Canvey with her on Fridays just as Irene had done. While Sue went shopping I would walk round the room with Ivy, identifying all the photographs on the wall or engaging in those circular repetitive conversations that are the mark of dementia. I got quite good at this – the thing to do is to go with it and follow the circles round and round, and not lose patience with the repeated questions. As far as that person knows, each conversation is new, so just sit back and enjoy the roundabout. Every turn means a signal or a wave of the hand to somebody who is losing contact, isolated and lost.

Although Ivy had known Sue for many years, she was no longer quite sure who she was and once, when Sue had gone out shopping, Ivy said to me, 'Would you ever think of getting married again?' I said, 'No – would you?' and we both laughed. It was a rare moment of contact, like a bridge between our retreating worlds.

At other times I would take the bus to Canvey and spend the afternoon with Ivy. It was strange sitting in that place that had been like home to me when I was a teenager. Now only Ivy remained, and her welfare was in my hands. We would talk and look at photographs. We never mentioned Irene. I am sure that Ivy remembered her (though she was often puzzled by Jim's wristwatch), but I don't think I could have spoken her name without cracking up, so we were tacit on that subject.

When the social worker came at tea time, I would walk to the Haystack pub to take a drink. This corner of Canvey Island is still recognisable as the place I knew from my childhood, and after a large whisky, I would step on to the street and see the young people and remember me and Irene in that very place. This nostalgia felt rather pleasant, so I would step back in and have another couple of drinks – and then the misery would hit me. If a bus didn't come I would set off on foot across Canvey Island, stumbling through neighbourhoods of our youth all the way to Benfleet to get another drink and the bus back to my empty house in Southend.

At home it was easy to evoke Irene. I would imagine she was just outside the door, about to step into the room, and for a few moments I could feel her presence. Once, I was walking to the station down a street filled with cherry blossom. There was a woman walking towards me on the other side of the street. In the distance, she bore a resemblance to Irene and I amused myself by imagining it was she, coming to meet me. As we drew closer, the illusion broke down and this stranger passed by. I could see the street winding away among the blossoms and I thought, 'I could walk down this road for ever, for a million miles, and I would never, never meet her.' I would look up at the stars and realise that in

143

all the gulfs and light years of the cosmos she was nowhere to be found. The Moon looked like a cold lump of mud in the sky.

I started playing gigs again. What else could I do? Drive down the motorway to some town. Get to the venue, take the guitars out of the boot of the car and go in. People testing microphones (one thing about sound checks is you learn to say 'One, two; one, two' in various languages – my favourite is the Finnish, '*Yksi kaksi; yksi kaksi*'). Do the sound check – this usually involves banging on some drums and then playing a song. If everything is working OK then that's it – I don't like to spend too long playing to an empty room, and a three-piece band is easy to balance.

Then there's a couple of hours to kill in the dressing room – it's my habit to pace round in circles, always in an anti-clockwise direction. Why this should be I do not know – I've tried forcing myself to go clockwise, but as soon as my attention wanders, my feet return to their habitual direction. I've even checked it out in the southern hemisphere, and in Sydney and in Auckland it's just the same, so it can't be the Coriolis effect. I must have one leg shorter than the other. And all this time thinking about Irene.

Gigs were usually at weekends, so I was able to visit Ivy during the week. I was always grateful to Sue for the lifelong friendship she had given Irene, and now she continued that friendship by caring for Ivy. Time went by. Sue helped me and the boys put up decorations and make Christmas dinner. Again it was strange sitting in that room, so familiar from my teenage years, with my own sons, while Ivy, once so vital, had become a confused old lady. And no one said a word about the ghost of Irene all around us.

Winter turned to spring and spring turned to summer, and I carried on playing gigs around the UK and in Europe and Japan. All along that endless highway, in a kind of daze. Thinking about Irene.

Then came a day when I returned from a tour of Spain to find that Ivy had been taken into Runwell psychiatric hospital. She now needed twenty-four-hour care, so we found a place for her at a pleasant home in Southend that specialised in dementia care. With a very heavy heart I went with Matthew in his car to take Ivy from the hospital to the care home. As they brought her out through the hospital doors, she saw me and said, 'Oh, I'm glad you've come – you'll look after me.' She had recognised that bloke dressed in black. Going along in the car she said, 'Where are we?' Matthew said, 'Near Basildon,' and Ivy said, 'Not that I know where I'm going.' She knew she wasn't going home.

We took her to the care home and settled her in. And in that home where time stood still, Ivy slowly faded away, forgot everything, and died.

The Reverend Brenda held a funeral service at Canvey Island Methodist Church. Me, Sue, Matthew, Simon and the few surviving members of the Methodist Young Wives' Club. We took the coffin to Southend crematorium, and the four of us and the Reverend Brenda saw her off.

Irene had left instructions that her mother's ashes should be interred in the Knight family grave in the churchyard on Canvey Island, and after a week or so I called the undertakers to arrange it. I went over to Canvey at the appointed time and walked to the grave. A small hole had been dug, but there was nobody there. There was a burial taking place over on the other side of the graveyard.

I walked across to the undertakers' office next to the church. A woman came out and I said, 'Er . . . Ivy Knight?' She thought for a moment then said, 'Oh yes,' and walked out the back, returning with a little wooden casket which she placed in my arms. I said, 'Er . . . ?' and she said 'Oh, there will be somebody over there.'

So I walked back to the graveyard. The burial party were leaving and I walked among them, carrying Ivy in my arms. This graveyard, surrounded now by housing estates where once had been open fields, was familiar to me from my childhood. There was a gravestone near the church door inscribed with the name *Beckwith* and two hands clasping in farewell. This image of death and separation used to fascinate me when I was a child. There was something tender and affectionate in the gesture of the hands, and I imagined Beckwith bidding Beckwith a fond farewell for ever and ever. Behind the church was the grave of The Coastguard's Daughter – we are not told why she died so young, but I would picture her in a sou'wester holding aloft a hurricane lamp and bravely facing storm and shipwreck.

The graveyard was now empty and I walked towards the Knights' grave. Me – the teenage boy who had stepped into the Knights' bungalow all those years ago, and now I was carrying the last of them to rest. It was an intense and reverent feeling and I was pleased the undertaker hadn't shown up.

There was no shovel by the grave, so I put her in the ground and buried her with my bare hands. I stood for a while in silence and turned to go. Just then the undertaker himself came running across the field. I waved my hand to him and said, 'It's all right, mate. It's sorted.'

CHAPTER 18

Time went by and time went by. Out on the road doing gigs, Irene always on my mind. At home I was living alone and my house was turning into a slum, disorder everywhere. I would shoot the place up with my air pistol – no light bulb or bric-a-brac was safe from my marksmanship. This state of disintegration suited my state of mind. I would see loose leaves from a diary I had kept in 1974 (when the Feelgoods first were happening) scattered and kicking around the floor – I had kept the pages for all these years and now I watched them disappear and thought, 'Let it go, let it go.' I used to refer to the house as my 'entropy tank'. Life without Irene was just time to be passed. I passed some of it looking through telescopes.

I first became interested in astronomy in 1979 when I went to Australia with Ian Dury and the Blockheads. We had quite an arduous flight and arrived in Melbourne thoroughly jet-lagged. (I never used to believe in jet-lag, thinking it was something that happened to straight people who weren't used to staying up all night, but this flight had been long and the jet-lag was on me. It's quite a feeling – one minute you're speeding around, encountering people in hotel corridors at three in the morning, then you're hit by a thousand-ton sleepiness, and then you get enthusiastic again. Jet-lag – if you could buy it, I would definitely keep some around for special occasions.) It was night-time when we checked into the hotel and the thought came into my head that we were in the southern hemisphere, under different stars.

I immediately made my way to the roof of the hotel, where there was a swimming pool, and lay down on one of those relaxer things to begin my observations. Not only were the stars very different, but there were many more of them than I was used to, and furthermore they were coloured red and gold. And they were moving. I realised that what I was looking at were fireflies attracted by the swimming-pool lights. I also realised that I knew nothing about the southern sky – or indeed the northern – and I went back downstairs.

A few years later I was booked to play a tour of New Zealand, which would give me another chance to see the southern sky. Not wishing to repeat the Melbourne debacle, I decided to learn a bit about the northern sky before returning to the Antipodes. Instead of learning to identify the constellations, I concerned myself with this question – is the Moon upside down in New Zealand? It's a difficult problem – I couldn't find any mention of it in books of astronomy. I thought and thought – I even tried standing on my head and thinking about it – but there was no solution. I would just have to go and see for myself. But first I would have to familiarise myself with the Moon as seen from home, so I started looking at it whenever I could and memorising its features.

While I was doing this it occurred to me that the Moon is by far the most familiar object in the universe. Every single human being who ever lived with eyes to see has gazed at that thing – cavemen and pharaohs, Greek philosophers, and everybody reading these words. Everybody. There's nothing else like that.

When I reached New Zealand, however, there was no moon to see and for the first week or so of the tour the skies were overcast. Some of the gigs we played were in ballrooms at hotels along the highway – this was good because your hotel room was only a couple of minutes from the stage and you could use it as a dressing room. One evening I had come off stage and was walking across to the hotel. I was still carrying my guitar. I turned a corner and there before me the great disc of the full Moon was rising. It was upside down.

Back at home I continued to watch the Moon, especially when I discovered that ordinary binoculars can give spectacular views of its scarred surface. Then I pointed my binoculars at the planet Jupiter. I was thrilled to see a tiny disc with the four pinpoints of the Galilean moons strung out on either side. This was the sight that told Galileo that the earth was not at the centre of everything and changed our understanding of the universe for ever. Every clear night

I would look at Jupiter and watch how the moons moved round it.

But there was one sight I wanted to see that binoculars would not show – the rings of Saturn. For this you need a telescope.

I ordered a small astronomical telescope. This was a battery-powered thing with a computer that would point it at any object in the sky. At night I would carry the telescope and tripod into the back garden and set it up. Aligning the telescope involved pointing it manually at two different stars. Sometimes these stars would be hidden behind the leaves of trees in the garden and my method of dealing with this was not to select differently aligned stars, but to leap up and tear down the offending branches. I wondered what neighbours might think should they look out of their windows in the small hours and see me in my garden jumping up and down pulling branches off trees.

It was nearly dawn. I had been up all night and the telescope's batteries were dead. There was a bright star rising over the housetops and I knew it was Saturn. I pointed the telescope that way, looked through the eyepiece and started randomly sweeping the sky. It's almost impossible to find a star in this way without the computer, but suddenly an unmistakable object shot across the field of view. Like a perfect tiny jewel, it was my first sight of Saturn. I gasped and returned the planet to the centre of view. There it flew in a blue dawn sky, tilted to show the famous rings. Saturn.

My little telescope developed a fault after a while and the shop said they couldn't fix it and would give me my money

151

back. I was having none of this and asked what was the next step up towards a real grown-up telescope.

And so it was that I took possession of a twelve-inch Meade LX200. This was big and it was heavy. There was no chance of carrying it back and forth from the garden – in fact the instruction manual contains the following advice: *Two or more people should always be used to move the telescope. Disregard of the above warning could result in serious injury or death.* Grim pictures of my friends finding me one morning beneath the telescope like a squashed hedgehog. But my house has a flat roof. What else was there to do but haul the thing aloft? I made sure there were plenty of helpers and we all survived.

The best plan with a large telescope is to set the thing up and then leave it permanently in place – this avoids the necessity of aligning it every time. It also means that the telescope must be protected from the elements. I kept mine covered with tarpaulins, but this wasn't very neat or reliable. Eventually, using tarpaulin and plenty of gaffer tape, I made a fitted cover for it. The cover took the form of a seven-foot green condom, flared at the base to accommodate the tripod.

When darkness fell I would emerge from my trap-door, pull off the cover and there was my telescope ready to go. There was a problem when I had finished – it was impossible to reach up and simply put this long condom over the tele-scope, and I adopted the method of getting inside the thing, walking it over to the 'scope, putting it over the 'scope, then crouching down and crawling out from underneath. This was awkward, and on frosty nights when the cover was frozen stiff, something of an ordeal. My paranoia also gave rise to fears that those same neighbours who had observed my antics pulling leaves off trees would look out of their windows and see a seven-foot-tall green alien stumbling about on my roof before engulfing the telescope.

Eventually I decided to house my (now massive 14-inch) telescope in a dome. This is made of fibreglass, delivered in prefabricated sections. It consists of a circular wall with a domed roof that turns on a roller track. I built the cylindrical lower section myself, but needed assistance to lift the revolving dome into place. For some days I would go up to the roof and stand inside the topless dome like a child in a playpen. Still wishing for total discretion, I decided to thwart the curiosity of my neighbours and complete the construction under the cover of darkness. That way, the dome would appear one morning without commotion and hopefully pass unnoticed.

Round about this time I took up cycling. At first I practised riding around at three or four o'clock in the morning, when the streets were deserted. On one of these early expeditions I rode up the street that runs parallel to mine. There is a gap between two houses on the street where you can look through to the back of my house, and I wanted to see how conspicuous my dome was. I rode slowly along hunting for the place – 'This is it – no, the next one . . . ' By the time I found the spot I was riding very slowly – I saw the dome, it was huge and shining white in the darkness. My astonishment was interrupted by the realisation that I had slowed down too much and was actually going to fall off. It's really hard to fall off a bike without making a noise – basically you've just got to fall without flailing about, and so I did, toppling over in slow motion. The side of my face made contact with terra firma and somehow seemed to keep falling so that my cheek was ground into the pavement. But I made not a sound.

I got up and looked around. The street was dark and silent and no one had witnessed my mishap. I pushed the bike home.

I've got another story involving astronomy, cycling and Newton's first law of motion . . .

I had been up all night making my observations and morning was breaking, so I switched off the telescope and went downstairs. (That's the astronomy bit.) I had a cup of coffee, then found that I needed some Rizlas. It was broad daylight by then but still very early and no one about, so I set off on my bike for the 24-hour shop.

In the shop I thought I might as well buy some provisions, including milk, bread and a jar of marmalade. The man put my purchases in one of those extraordinarily delicate blue plastic bags. It was already stretching as I walked out of the shop and I was forced to gather the whole bundle in my arms. In doing so, the top burst off the marmalade and it began pouring down my front. I was still in full view of the shopkeeper, so I kept walking steadily until I was out of sight. I disposed of the marmalade jar – most of its contents were soaking into my shirt – and mounted my bike. The bag had disintegrated, so I balanced the groceries in the crook of my arm and set off.

When I reached the top of my street my arm was aching, so I stopped and transferred the pile of items to my left arm. Now, my street is on what we in Essex are pleased to call a hill – that is, it declines from the horizontal by a few degrees – so I could freewheel the last leg of my journey. So I go sailing down the street . . . I'm accelerating . . . here comes my house . . . At this point I realise that using my right hand to control the bike means that I can only operate the front brake. Any cyclist will appreciate the peril I was in. A couple of dabs on the brake emphasised this. My house was racing towards me – what could I do? The voice of reason would have said, 'Drop the groceries, they're gonna hit the ground anyway,' but I had reached my house so I jammed on the brake.

Newton's first law of motion states that an object will continue to move in a straight line until acted on by a contrary force. The bike, acted on by the brake, experienced a sudden deceleration, while I continued in a straight line over the handlebars and ended up sprawled on my back in the middle of the street with the groceries strewn about me. As I said, it was broad daylight but still very early. I looked around and found that once again I had escaped unobserved, but at any moment one of those inquisitive neighbours could look out and my credibility would be damaged beyond repair.

I got to my feet and gathered up my bike and the scattered groceries. I was in considerable pain – in fact I believe I was actually whimpering as I dragged myself indoors. I lay on the floor for some time before realising that I had forgotten to buy the Rizlas.

CHAPTER 19

In 2007 I was told that Julien Temple was going to make a film about Canvey Island and the origins of Dr Feelgood. I knew about Julien's work, but I had never met him, and I wondered how he was going to do such a thing. Lee Brilleaux was dead; Sparko and The Big Figure retired from music; Dr Feelgood forgotten. We had existed in the days before video and there was little archive footage.

His first move was impressive. He arranged to film interviews with me, Sparko and Figure in the Canvey Island oil terminal. At night. Live footage of Dr Feelgood from 1975 was to be projected on to the big oil tanks as a backdrop. The oil terminal was a place I had known all my life. Growing up on Canvey Island you were always aware of its presence, even when you couldn't see it. But nobody, apart from workers, ever went in there, so it was always mysterious. To stand in this sacred druidical grove of oil tanks, while huge silent moving images of us in our heyday lit up the darkness, was mysterious indeed. Those images – Lee, Sparko, Figure and me with the world at our feet, setting out on that long highway . . . Powerful memories gripped me – what a kick it all was and what friends we had all been. How did it go so wrong? Thirty-five years later, this night was bringing it all back home to Canvey Island.

The film took some time to complete, being beset by financial problems, but *Oil City Confidential* was released in 2009 to great acclaim. I went to the premiere at the South Bank – normally I'm leery of watching myself on film, but of course I had to be there at the premiere, so I drank some champagne and went in. The film was brilliant. What was particularly intriguing to me was to see the 1975 live footage up on a big screen with the music loud. It was the first time I had ever really seen Dr Feelgood. I was sitting next to my son Simon as we watched this thing I had done long before he was born and I couldn't resist nudging him and mouthing, 'Pretty good!'

Things were looking up for my band – the success of *Oil City Confidential* was bringing in bigger audiences to our gigs – there was a whole generation who had never known Dr Feelgood apart from the risible travesty that had been masquerading under that name for years, and the film went some way to re-establish a reputation that had been lost in the punk revolution. And I was the only exponent left of that thing that we did.

By then Norman and I had recruited Dylan Howe to play the drums with us. Dylan (another ex-Blockhead) is a brilliant drummer and his playing transformed and revitalised the band. I was getting real kicks playing and we were packing out our regular venues like the Half Moon in Putney and the 100 Club, as well as gigs in Europe, Ireland, Scandinavia and, of course, Japan. I think I was coming back to life, but still in love with Irene; still missing her.

Then I was asked to audition for a film part. I had never done any acting and I was interested. They told me that the film was to be for an American TV series called *Game of Thrones*. I thought this was maybe going to be something like *Xena: Warrior Princess* and I was pretty keen to do it – maybe I would get a leather jacket out of it. I was the only person at the audition, just me and a bloke with a video camera. He told me that the character I was to play was thoroughly evil and malicious. More importantly he had had his tongue cut out – this meant there were no lines to learn. He read some script to me and I had to register hatred and violence. I can do that. I got the job.

When I went to Belfast, where the film company had their headquarters at the old Harland and Wolff shipyard, I quickly realised that this was something more than *Xena: Warrior Princess*. There were sheds full of exquisitely made, intricate suits of armour, racks of fearsome weapons, carved wooden artefacts. I was given a costume of rough cloth covered with chain mail. It was the real deal, made of metal and stretching from my neck to my wrists and my knees. It was really heavy. On top of it was a leather jerkin which covered most of the chain mail – why couldn't they just have given me chain-mail sleeves? But everything on *Game of Thrones* was authentic, including the double-handed sword slung on my back. With my mute character, I had little to do but glare at people (including women and children) and generally hang round waiting for the King to tell me to behead or mutilate someone. I was a very bad dude.

Right from the outset I enjoyed this fantasy. Wearing authentic-seeming medieval clothes and carrying heavy weapons, it was easy to participate in this impossible world – beautifully carved carts and furniture and incongruous lighting sheets up in the trees. And hundreds of cars parked, and people with megaphones and names written on the back of their chairs. This was a big production. I had a caravan with my name and a star on it. I got to meet some of the other actors and realised that they're good people who like a laugh and not the luvvies of *Private Eye* notoriety. They've just got a different way of looking at things.

My dumb killer was an easy part to play, especially as the real actors were so friendly and helpful. In fact the whole operation, from costume to caterers to actors, was carried out in an atmosphere of enjoyment, even when there were problems – 'Hurry up now! We're losing the light!'

It was all very different from staging a rock 'n' roll show. For one thing you start very early in the morning in order to catch the light; film people are up and doing while rockers are just crawling into bed. There's also the sheer numbers of people involved. You can put on a big rock show with a couple of dozen roadies and technicians, but there are hundreds involved in a film production. Just look at the credits at the end of any movie – so many jobs. (I was fascinated to see continuity people making sure the candles remained the same length between takes.) And the whole thing was done with military precision. A big rock show is slammed together during the afternoon, while between takes on a film set there is a frenzy of activity, dozens of people all with precise roles – like a pit stop in a Formula One race.

The first scene I took part in was set in a torchlit hall, where Sean Bean (playing Lord Eddard Stark) was arguing with the King. The room was filled with armoured knights and warriors. Everything looked absolutely real – even the cameras were largely out of sight. And it was real. I completely felt myself to be a warrior in this fantasy world, something I hadn't experienced since childhood. At one point Sean (who had greeted me when I first came to the set – what a gent) spoke some scornful words to me and I had to react with silent anger. This too felt real to me – I could have hung out day and night in that dream world.

When *Game of Thrones* was first shown its audience must have been bigger than everybody I had ever played to in my life put together. My face was on the big billboards advertising the show. I began to get fan mail, largely from America, praising my brief appearances as Ser Ilyn Payne, and people would stop me in the street, talking about *Game of Thrones* rather than my years of musical endeavour (sometimes both).

I also took part in the second series, some of which was filmed in Malta. I remember looking across the Mediterranean at the beautiful old town and my heart aching and aching for Irene.

Going on stage and playing gigs provided some respite from my grief, but I continued to think of Irene all the time. Walk

onstage to a welcoming cheer from the crowd. 'Good evening.
One, two, three, four –' Always a jolt when Norman's bass
kicks in. Start to move with the rhythm and off you go – your
everyday personality drops away and you become this creature
making this noise, singing these words.

> *I wanna live the way I like – sleep all the morning, go*
> *and get my fun at night*

And the first song runs straight into the second. Catch
your breath –

> *Take a look around you and you'll find out where you*
> *are*
> *Walking on the edge*

– and that's the second number. Big loud chord. Blam! . . .
The people are cheering and you're saying *thank you, thank
you*. One, two, three, and

> *I have got my eyes on you*

Now you're talking about some doe-eyed girl from long
ago, she had this compulsive neurosis –

> *You can walk in a zig-zag, trying not to step on the*
> *squares,*
> *Close your eyes every time that you climb my stairs*
> *You can shimmy when you put on your shoes – I just*
> *don't care –*

– but right now, you're playing your guitar – *jab, jab* – as you move across the stage. (Don't slip over in the pool of sweat around Norman's feet!)

Slow down. Reggae. Minor key.

I wanna go down to the open ground
I can see the picture's turning round
And though I know I'll be out there on my own
This time I don't care if I drown
Doctor Dupree won't write no more for me
And I'm getting tired of coming down

– old memories of despair from long ago. But it doesn't hurt now – it's just a picture. (Between the railway line and Benfleet Creek there is a big swathe of flat land. Sitting there looking west to the refinery towers and all that tract that fronts the falling sun, you can think about suicide.) Start again.

Watch out if you think you're going places
People sometimes take you by surprise
And if you ain't got fifty different faces
You've got to be a master of disguise
Ah, watch out! – you're gonna find out
Find out for yourself, boy, what's going on.
Ice on the motorway – you can't go that way
You just gotta walk, that's all, come on.

– still thinking about Irene, but she's distant, like the rest of the world. (I don't like to talk between numbers, but play the show non-stop. If there is a technical problem which delays things for a few seconds, I'm suddenly transformed into a geezer in black holding a guitar, and I wait impatiently to plunge back into the illusion and the music.)

Come on, come on, keep the beat – the next one starts with the guitar. Steady. *Chuggah chuggah chuggah chuggah.* Don't rush. Feel it.

I got a girl from Cairo
Descended from a Pharaoh
Gazing over deserts from the waters of the Nile
Pharaoh kept his secret hid, buried in his pyramid
But she can keep it all behind her smile.

Then the next one, the next one, rolling like a train:

My last rider – don't ask why,
She used to drive me crazy –
She kept on driving till the tank ran dry, the tank ran
  dry. Yeah.

Take it down, wander about the stage, look up into the lights. Take it way down low.

Then: 'On the bass – Norman Watt-Roy!' Big cheer from the crowd, they're all shouting his name – they love him. Come on Norman, hit me with your rhythm stick! And he plays in his own lagoon of perspiration, hunched over his bass as though he wants to strangle it.

Applause, applause. 'On the drums – Dylan Howe!' Snap,

snap. What's he gonna do? Phrases, breaks and paradiddles, different every night. Drum solos are generally crass and should be avoided, but Dylan's got all these tricks up his sleeve and you wave your arm and the people all cheer. Dylan Howe! Dylan Howe!

Now we're getting near the close.

'Back In The Night'. 'She Does It Right'. Right back where I started from. Every time I start 'Back In The Night', I remember that night in our bungalow when Irene went off to see to the baby and I started writing the song, only to have it dissed by the rest of the band in the morning. Different songs put you in mind of different things. Some songs don't mean anything at all.

Waving bye bye. Goodnight. Goodnight.

Walking off stage, sadness comes back, pouring down on me.

CHAPTER 20

Some time in 2012 I noticed a lump in my stomach. It was about the size of a plum and kind of amorphous – it would change shape, sometimes growing longer, sometimes disappearing altogether. It didn't hurt and I decided to treat it by ignoring it and hoping it would go away. At the end of the year, when my son Matthew visited me, he saw this thing and took me straight to Southend General Hospital.

There were days of scans and X-rays and fear. Then I went in for a biopsy, which involves snipping off a sample of tissue for examination. I remember being pushed along on a trolley, the long hospital corridors unwinding like a movie in front of me. In the biopsy room I lay looking at the intent face of a young Chinese student as he stared into his monitor screen and pushed the needle into me. A doctor beside the bed spoke reassuring words as she held my hand. I remembered Afghanistan's plains. I remembered strutting and fretting my hour upon the stage in front of crowds of thousands. Now I lay like a frightened child squeezing a motherly hand for comfort. The doctor says, 'There will be a loud sound – don't be alarmed.' This is the sound of the jaws at the end of the needle cutting off the sample. Snap! Not pleasant. I held the doctor's hand while they snapped a second time.

A couple of days later I'm sitting in a room with Matthew and a doctor and a nurse. Apprehension. The doctor says, 'You've got this mass in your stomach and pancreas.' (I know.) 'Unfortunately we cannot operate on this.' (First warning.) And then the words, 'You've got cancer.'

The universe changed for ever. I felt absolutely calm. All the worry and fear of the past few days seemed to lift from me. Now I knew.

They told me the cancer was incurable and terminal. I felt absolutely calm.

We walked out of the hospital. It was a bright winter's day. I looked up at the bare branches of the trees against the sky – they looked beautiful and with a rush of emotion I suddenly felt intensely alive. My existence was irrevocably coming to an end but here and now I was alive in the sunlight. Everything around me looked sharp and vibrant. I felt free. Free from the future and the past, free from everything but this moment I was in.

By the time I got home I was almost ecstatic. I wondered if this was some kind of shock reaction, soon to collapse into horror, but I didn't come down. Walking round my transformed house, curious about this new universe I had stepped into, I called my best mate Mickey Fawcett to tell him the news. (Mike and I had been close friends for a long time. Over the years we have shared many ups and downs – mostly ups. When she was dying, Irene said to me, 'He really is your friend, you know' as if she were consigning me to his care.)

Mike was obviously shocked and upset when I told him, but I spoke with the absolute calm I had felt in the hospital, as if I was talking about somebody else. I sat down and thought – where was I? I was in another universe certainly, in a detached, elevated state, as if I were in an impenetrable bubble that cut me off from the world around me. It was hard to realise the fact that I was fatally ill. I didn't feel ill. The tumour didn't hurt and I was showing no symptoms of sickness, so cancer was an idea rather than a disease making its presence felt.

I was in a hospital ward, looking down a long perspective of beds. Everything was grey; there was no colour. In every bed was an identical figure sitting bolt upright, staring ahead. They looked like eighteenth-century clerics in grey vestments. Sparse white locks covered their skulls. Their faces were stern, impassive; they stared grimly ahead as if contemplating some ancient and irredeemable catastrophe. I knew that these people were all suffering from an incurable and fatal disease. I walked to a bedside. The figure ignored me, remaining absolutely still. Suddenly he seized my wrist in an unshakeable grip. I tried to pull my wrist away but his grip was like iron. I shouted 'Let go of me!' He took no notice. My struggles were useless, he just kept staring ahead. I pleaded, 'Let me go and I'll give you a million pounds!' He did not respond, staring grimly ahead. Then I shouted 'Let me go

*or I'll kill you!' Blackness. I awoke with fear clutching my heart,
and I knew that I had a fatal cancer.*

I woke every day with this knowledge, though I didn't
usually dream about it. In fact, in my dreams I never had
cancer. Waking, there would be a few minutes of disbelief,
fear and then acceptance, and I would start another day
in this new world, isolated in my bubble. I had no fear
of death itself but I did dread the process of dying. I'm a
wimp when it comes to illness. The thought of lying on a
sickbed weak and nauseated, knowing that I would never
recover, but only descend into dissolution, wasn't one I
liked to dwell on. But right now, in the time that remained
to me, I felt fit and healthy and I wondered what to do.
Obviously I should enjoy the months that were left to me
as I best could.

I decided to accept absolutely the idea that my life was at
an end, and to waste none of my remaining time on false
hopes and disappointments, second opinions or miracle cures
(though I did enjoy internet reports that people showed me,
saying that high doses of cannabis had been found to have
anti-carcinogenic effects – I would happily research this). I
had money in the bank. I would spend it prodigally, doing
whatever I wanted, denying myself nothing.

A few days later, I went back to the hospital to hear a
more detailed account of my condition. They stressed at
the beginning that my cancer was inoperable and told me
that chemotherapy could only slow it down and not stop or
cure it. I had about ten months; with chemo, maybe a year.
It would be foolish to endure the agonies of chemotherapy

for the sake of a couple of extra months of illness, so I told them that I didn't want to lose my hair and declined that option. I was still feeling high and it was easy to be flippant. They said that the apparent good health I was currently experiencing might last for a few more months before the cancer struck, but they seemed to be telling me that I had less than a year to live.

I walked home, still feeling high. That night I went to London, where I was to get up and play a number with Madness at the O2. Backstage in my bubble, telling everybody I had cancer. Ironically, Suggs was just setting up his charity Pancreatic Cancer UK, with the aim of funding research to increase the survival rate from 3 per cent to 10 per cent. Too late for me. Laughing and joking backstage. Standing on stage looking across the vast audience and thinking it's funny how things turn out. All those roads, all those gigs, and now it's coming to an end, standing on this stage with the hand of death on my shoulder.

When I came offstage I met Martin Freeman and told him I had just been diagnosed with terminal cancer. Bit of a conversation-killer really.

Southend General had said they wanted to see me periodically and I'd made an appointment with a dietician. This wasn't a doctor, just a geek in a white coat. He weighed me and noted no loss of weight. I told him I was feeling fit and healthy, to which he said, 'Oh, that won't last long!' Well, thank you very much! I didn't go back to Southend General – I would wait until my final sickness began and they could give me morphine and sleeping pills.

*

The first thing I wanted to do was visit Japan, that place I had come to love so much, one last time and say goodbye to all my friends there. I wanted to share the trip with somebody, so I called my old friend Benjamin Tehoval in Brussels. Ben is a French blues musician, a one-man band. We had met him in the old days, Norman and Sav and I, when we were touring Spain. Arriving at a gig, we'd been backstage when the support band started their sound check. They struck up with '44 Blues', lurching into the song with a real blues feeling that is rarely heard. I said, 'These guys are great!' and rushed out to the stage to see them. 'They' turned out to be a skinny guy sitting with a guitar and a harmonica harness, playing a bass drum and cymbal with his left foot while his right performed a crazy dance across a set of bass pedals. He sang in a clear, plaintive, French-accented voice.

I loved this music, so we asked the promoter to add Ben to the bill on the rest of our tour. He began travelling with us and we struck up an immediate friendship. This was the beginning of thousands of miles of Spanish highways and gigs over the ensuing years, when Ben would open our show and share the driving with Sav.

Ben is a good guy to travel with; he has a real traveller's curiosity. He had always wanted to visit Japan, and we would spend time in Tokyo and the lovely cities Kyoto and Nara, riding first class on plane and bullet train and staying in fine hotels.

We had cancelled a gig we were due to play on Canvey Island after my diagnosis and we put a statement on the website apologising for this, and announcing my illness and my refusal of chemotherapy. The story started to get picked up in the mainstream press in the UK and abroad. By the time we arrived in Japan, the news was all over the internet and there was intense interest in my case. Twitter, twitter. We decided to play a couple of impromptu gigs in Tokyo and Kyoto to raise money for the Great Tsunami disaster fund. (I was later to receive a letter of thanks for this from the President of the Japanese Red Cross – one of many things I would never have expected in my life that were to crowd into these terminal months.)

At the Red Shoes club in Tokyo, Ben and I foregathered with Sheena and Makoto Ayukawa and their band the Rokkets and many other prominent Japanese musicians who wanted to take part. Although unadvertised, the gig had immediately sold out and TV monitor screens had been installed for the crowds outside in the street. Ben opened the show to a packed and emotional house. People were in tears, holding up signs with messages of love for me, and when I came on stage with Makoto and the Rokkets the place erupted. The gig was chaotic – Sheena got up to sing, and then a succession of guitarists and singers and drummers took the stage. The crowd surged and swayed, a sea of Japanese faces, many of them in tears. I'd always known my music was popular in Japan – we had played over the years to several generations of fans and always found a good audience – but here was an expression of personal affection I had never known existed. It was touching. Moving. At the end of the show I said, 'Goodnight and goodbye,' and my heart was full of gratitude and love for these people.

After the show I was given all kinds of groovy presents,

including a sackful of letters and a big Japanese flag covered with signatures and messages. The letters bore out the feeling of personal affection I had felt from the crowd. Many were in broken English, which made them all the more touching. There were people around the world who cared about me, and I could not let them down. I could never give way to fear and despair but should continue to face my coming death with a brave face. How do you give way to fear? Fall on the floor screaming, 'Help me! Help me!'? There is nobody who can help and nowhere to run to. You might as well relax and keep your cool – the end will come just the same.

> *If it be now, 'tis not to come.*
> *If it be not to come, it will be now.*
> *If it be not now, yet it will come.*

Then on the bullet train, past snow-clad Mount Fuji and on to Kyoto, ancient capital of Japan. It's pleasant to ride on the bullet train, with its luxurious seats and smooth, silent high-speed running. The destination announcements are made in clear euphonious female tones, the English parts with a soft Japanese/American accent – *Ladies and gentlemen, welcome to the Shinkansen. This is the Nozomi super express bound for Shin-Osaka. We will be stopping at Shinagawa, Shin-Yokohama, Nagoya, and Kyoto before arriving at Shin-Osaka terminal.* The lady appears at the entrance to the coach and bows to the passengers before wheeling in the refreshment trolley. (The Japanese practice of bowing is a wonderfully graceful and civilised thing. I remember once in Kyoto I was up in the early morning before the shops opened. I saw a small crowd gathering at the entrance to a big department store. Inside was a huge sales floor with many rows of counters. By each counter stood sales girls in uniform, their white-gloved hands folded. The manager came to open the door and as he did so these sales girls, all together, bowed to the first customers of the day. I flipped – I thought, 'Right, I'm gonna buy something in here!' Later, I excitedly described this spectacle to Keiko, and she said, 'Well, of course.' Of course. It was an everyday thing. But what a thing!)

We checked into my favourite hotel, the Monterey, and prepared for our visit to Kyoto. There are hundreds of temples and shrines in Kyoto and the surrounding hills. The city is built on a grid pattern, quite unlike the winding streets and lanes of Tokyo. Step out of the Monterey on to a busy main thoroughfare and you are just a few blocks away from the Terrimarche, a massive market made up of three long covered streets. Shops full of T-shirts, jewellery, exquisite art work, cheap toys, shoes, lacquerwork, wood carving, and more fish than you ever knew swam in the sea. And chemists and cafés, along with small temples and shrines with bells and statues and curving roofs. I had come to love these streets over the years, and walking there now, knowing that this would be the last time I would ever be there, was poignant, a mixture of sadness and deep friendship. For the last time, I was taking in the sights of this beautiful place. (One good thing about the rock 'n' roll road is that it takes you to all manner of exotic places where you aren't a tourist, you're there to work (ha! ha! – pretty good job!), so you can walk around feeling that you belong there, rather than just rubber-necking.)

Ben, Yuriko and I were eventually joined by Keiko, who had come from Nagoya, and Noriko, a long-time fan and friend. Noriko is a happy-natured person – being shy of speaking English (which she understands very well), she communicates by smiles, gestures, single words and enthusiasm.

We usually met in the Library at the Monterey, a quiet café-bar in the style of an 'English stately home'. Actually, it's pretty tasteful, being decorated with pukka tapestries, objets d'art and paintings along with the bookshelves. The Monterey also contains a full-size replica of a London church – the Japanese are fond of western-style white weddings with confetti and all the trappings, and these celebrations can follow a Buddhist or Shinto or civic solemnisation. Bells peal and the organ plays.

So it's a good place to congregate before setting out to see the sights. Cup of coffee, silver sugar-tongs, toastie, glass of Laphroaig. Over the years I had always sat at the same place, first table on the right, looking out at the street outside. Now, sitting in that same chair thinking about the places I wanted to visit and thinking about death, this room, these city streets, these well-remembered feelings – the room and the streets would remain, but not me.

I'm an atheist – I don't believe that consciousness survives death, nor can there be consciousness without a physical body. Consciousness is made up of thoughts – electrical impulses generated in the brain. Without a brain, no electrical impulses; without such impulses, no thoughts; without thoughts, no existence.

What is death like? What were you doing in 1929? Although this seems self-evident to me, it doesn't make the idea of death any less dreadful – the mind, capable of generating and contemplating ideas of infinite wonder and beauty in art and science and philosophy, capable perhaps of penetrating all the truth of the universe, balks at the idea of its own annihilation. We cannot grasp the thought of death, of infinite oblivion, any more than we can conceive the awful immensities and distances of the cosmos. The distance to the Moon? We can just about get hold of that – our old Transit van travelled that far in its lifetime – but a light year? It literally does not bear thinking about.

So there I was, sitting in my favourite place in the Library with the Relentless King of Terrors bearing down on me and feeling pretty good. Although I was mortally ill, I was still in no pain. Apart from occasional bleeding and perhaps nausea and the slowly growing lump in my stomach, the cancer was nothing more than a bad dream, and I was free to make the most of my remaining time. The elation I had experienced on receiving the diagnosis was still with me – the elation and the isolation, my bubble that protected me. Of course, this isolation might turn into the most terrible loneliness in the small hours of the night, and then I would know fear – those slow, lonely hours of helpless fear. But even that could be dealt with by picking up the phone and having a talk and a laugh with someone. The important thing was to live in the minute I was in, to accept my death as inevitable and to waste no time in struggling against it.

*

My Barclaycard, which was our sole source of finance, stopped working. We spent a day in the hotel trying to remedy it, talking to surly unhelpful people on the phone in Bombay and Huddersfield – we had friends at home in Southend going to my local Barclays branch, who were unable to account for or remedy the problem. There was a crazy scene in the hotel with a room full of Japanese friends. Ben and I were tripping, while Yuriko wielded her phone and laptop. She was getting really angry with the Barclays helpline and put out a message on Twitter and Facebook, telling people how Barclays were ruining my last holiday and asking them to complain.

Meanwhile we were hearing that the news of my cancer had somehow gone global and was being reported in the mainstream press in Europe and the USA – where it was said that 'actor' Wilko Johnson (I was better known in the States for my small part in *Game of Thrones* than as a musician) had declined treatment for terminal cancer.

It all seemed madly funny to me on that mild acid trip. Yuriko was shouting down the telephone, 'We're not in flucking China!' Barclays were sending messages offering help but not providing any.

Yuriko texted them, 'If you really want to help Wilko then give him back the twenty-four hours you have taken from his too short life.'

Newspapers across the globe were asking for interviews and we managed to block Barclays' phone lines with thousands of complaints from Japanese fans. Me, I laughed and laughed. I was out of my head. We all went down to the Library for a drink.

Out of the Library into the streets. A stroll or a taxi ride will carry you to some of the most exquisite buildings in the world – the Kiyomizu-dera, the great Toji pagoda, the Emperor's palace where they trim the lawns with scissors. All so tranquil – though we did enjoy (if not comprehend) Yuriko's vigorous rebuke of a gatekeeper at the palace who had been less than polite to Ben and me. I think he'd objected to *gaijin* profaning the Emperor's grounds. Come on man! It's all a long time ago. If you wanna come over to Essex some time we'll show you some proper bad manners.

Come to think of it, that was the only display of impoliteness I have ever been subjected to in all my time in Japan. Must be some kind of Zen.

The Sanjusangendo temple is a long hall in which stand a thousand life-size figures of the bodhisattva Kannon. Each of these statues is unique, a masterpiece of medieval wood carving covered in gold leaf. The figures stand in ranks on a long wooden terrace, and in the centre of this great choir is the colossal seated figure of the bodhisattva Kannon herself, with her thousand arms and serene Buddha-face looking down with compassion for all living beings. The Buddha's smile of understanding and acceptance is the perfect expression of the state I wanted to try and achieve – to be aware that you are just one of the untold millions of human beings who ever lived – to see yourself *sub specie aeternitatis*.

At Kiyomizu temple, which looks down on Kyoto, there is a pool of water with squares of rice paper piled by it. You write down your troubles and put the paper into the water, where it dissolves. I drew a crab on my piece of paper and watched it melt away. Kiyomizu-dera is a wonderful place of pagodas and curving tiled roofs, with steep slopes to climb, water to drink from long ladles, Buddhas in secluded places, a mysterious rabbit, a path where lovers can walk with their eyes closed to a special stone which brings true love, all set in beautiful trees among the hills. I liked the rice-paper cure. If only . . .

Walking in these places, knowing I was going to die, was like a dream. As if I had dreamed all the pagodas and Buddhas and temples and shrines – they were a transient shadow, soon to be taken from me for ever. I was drifting among them like a ghost.

One day we went up the hills to the Kurama temple. It was very tranquil – you could hear the birds whistling, and maybe a monk sweeping up. There is a balcony there that looks down the valley. I was alone, and I stood looking and thinking. What about? Death, probably. Down the valley a fine powdery snow was falling. As I looked the sun shone through and turned the snow to gold. This vision, more intense than any dream, hypnotised me. Golden snow, slowly falling between the trees. I wondered how I could keep this image in my memory, then remembered that I had no time to keep it for. I would have to experience it in that moment I was in. That was how I had to live my life now – in the moment. And I did it. The golden snow was falling, slowly falling, for ever and ever in that moment among the trees, and God, I was grateful to be alive.

Down in the city is another of Kyoto's wonders – the club Taku Taku. This is an old wooden building lost in a back street. It was once a *sake* distillery and is now one of the best gigs in the world. Taku Taku is presided over by Mr Mizushima, a sweet taciturn guy who I call 'my brother' because he bears a resemblance to Malcolm, almost like a Japanese version of him. When there is a gig at Taku Taku they paint the name of the artist on a board and nail it up outside, then afterwards they nail the board up inside the club. So it is that the walls of this little room are covered with some of the greatest names in music – John Lee Hooker, Dr John, the Staple Singers, Son House, Albert King, the Neville Brothers, Screaming Jay Hawkins, Bo Diddley, the Pirates and many more (including my humble self). The room gets packed and there is a wild atmosphere.

There are also quieter nights, when Mr Mizushima's band Porollys plays (he's the drummer). I went one night with Ben, Keiko, Noriko and Yuriko to see them play. They did a great version of 'Blueberry Hill' – it moved me almost to tears. There were just a few people in the club, human beings making that lovely sound and other human beings sitting there digging it. There was no harm in that room. I felt like an alien observer: 'What are these creatures doing? There are four of them making a noise and some others watching and swaying their bodies in time. But why? What are they doing? What are they making?'

'Nothing. They're just enjoying themselves.'

What incredible creatures.

We played another gig for the disaster relief fund at Taku Taku – me, Ben and a whole bunch of Japanese musicians. The place was packed to overflowing, and everybody there knew of my illness – knew that I had come to say goodbye.

The dressing room at Taku Taku is on the upper floor, a loft reached by a small open staircase. A gangway leads along the side of the room to the stage, somewhat after the manner of the Japanese *kabuki* theatre, so you walk down the steps at the back of the room, along the gangway and on to the stage. A better entrance couldn't be devised. As I stepped out on to the stairway I looked down into that room packed with people and the place erupted into a beautiful pandemonium – arms were reaching out to me, faces streaming with tears, rapturous acclaim. Oh, it felt so good – it felt so good – walking along the gangway to the stage – I was smiling and waving – the uproar grew and grew – on to the stage – plugging in my guitar – then bang into the show. I was flying high, looking out across the crowd – bang, bang, bang. You can't buy that feeling anywhere on earth.

The show was great. I can't remember much, just a blur of different musicians getting up and playing, the crowd in a constant uproar laughing and crying. As we left the stage and walked back up the staircase I waved goodbye, the whole crowd waving back – it was very moving, but I didn't feel sad – I just thought as I made my exit, to the cheers and the applause, 'This is great show business.'

Upstairs in the loft dressing room after the show there were journalists interviewing us and people filming – people crowding round me, shaking my hand, bowing, many with tears in their eyes. I was still high and happy from the show. I found myself consoling people, telling them everything was all right. It's enjoyable being the centre of attention, I was smiling at everyone. I can't help it, I really get a kick out of flattery and this was supercharged. Every eye in the room was on me and I was beaming like a lighthouse. So much noise. Protected by the dream-like elation that had been my state of mind ever since my diagnosis, my ego fed on this martyrdom. I felt like Gandhi at a Christmas party. Then a photographer told me that she was suffering from breast cancer. Complicated emotions filled me. We embraced. In that crowded, noisy room a sudden closeness and sympathy beyond words penetrated my armour.

The next day Keiko returned home to Nagoya. We stood on the street where her taxi waited, saying goodbye for ever. Yes, for ever. I was unlikely to return to Japan in the few months remaining to me and I would never see this dear friend again. (Well, probably – what with Skype and cheap flights, you couldn't be absolutely sure, but it felt pretty heavy.) All those years . . .

That evening Ben, Yuriko, Noriko and I sat in the restaurant across the street from the Monterey. Around midnight, Noriko had to go off for the night shift in the 7/11 store where she worked. Another lachrymose valediction.

In the early, early morning a cab took us to Osaka airport. We were just going through the departure gate when Ben said, 'Look.' It was Noriko – she had somehow come straight from work in Kyoto to see us off. We walked across to the barrier. Noriko was insisting in her broken English that we should return to Kyoto in April for cherry-blossom time. What could I say? I knew the cancer would be hitting me by then. But I promised her that if I was still on my feet we would see the cherry blossom one more time . . .

*

181

Back home in my empty house I crawled into an unmade bed to sleep off the jet lag.

I woke with the shivering fits, sweating, nausea, vomiting, diarrhoea. There was blood.

'Oh, no – not already! No! No!' Reality shoves its cold hand into my bubble of serenity and shakes me like a rag doll. When I had stopped vomiting I went to my bed to try and calm down. Death – at least it had spared me for my last trip to Japan, and I had been wise to go there straight away. But this looked like the end – what a disappointment! I felt miserable, I felt resigned, I felt a kind of gladness that it would soon be over.

I lay there following several trains of thought. Was this the onset of cancer? It seemed rather abrupt, and they had told me that symptoms would appear gradually, with weight loss and nausea increasing over a period of weeks or months. Still, what did they know? Of course, I feared the worst. I phoned Mike. When he arrived he was shocked by the sight of me. He told me later that I looked shrunken and shrivelled away, as if I had actually grown smaller in size. He went and got me a bowl of soup (probably to prevent me from disappearing altogether). It was very palatable and settled my stomach – in fact within an hour I had made a complete recovery.

So, not cancer then – a microwaved 'cottage pie' fell under suspicion – but it was the first occurrence of a problem that would plague me during these terminal months: every time I got a cold, or an upset stomach, or a headache,

I would fear that the tumour was beginning its deadly work. There was absolutely no way round this, so every minor ailment came freighted with fear and anxiety. I would tell myself, 'Right, if this is another false alarm I'm never going to fall for it again ...' And all this time the lump in my stomach was growing bigger.

CHAPTER 21

While I was in Japan, the story of my illness had been reported internationally, and back at home I was interviewed by all the UK press – the *Guardian*, the *Sun*, the *Sunday Times*, the *Mirror*, you name it – as well as radio and TV. I don't know what gave rise to this widespread interest – whether it was that I had made my illness public, or that I had declined treatment, or the attitude I was expressing. Probably a combination of all three. Anyway, amid all this publicity, and with my health not broken down yet, I decided I would make a farewell tour of the UK. We found several venues that could be booked at short notice and set up the tour.

My ambition and hope at the time was simply that my health would hold up long enough for me to play these dates. I knew Ian Dury and Lee Brilleaux had performed farewell shows when they were very sick, but I didn't want to do that – I wanted to go out with all guns blazing. Interest in my case had continued to grow, and when we announced the farewell tour the gigs immediately sold out.

There was another round of international newspaper and radio interviews, an appearance on breakfast TV. People were greeting me and shaking my hand on the street. Famous – it felt pretty good, even though it was only for a short time. Maybe I'll get an obituary in the *Guardian* like Lee.

I began to encounter cranks who would approach me with miracle cures that they had invented, telling me I must live on an all-cabbage diet, or plug myself into the AC electric mains, or turn to Jesus in order to effect a cure. These people could be insistent and very annoying. Did they not realise that I had troubles of my own and no time to spare on their lunacies? I was usually quite sharp in my replies to these insults to my intelligence. Other well-meaning people would say, 'Oh, my cousin was given ten months to live and she's still alive after two years!' I know they meant well, but I had a large and visibly growing tumour, and of course their words brought no comfort at all.

I was, I suppose, feeling good all this time. My normal state of mind, a fairly miserable one punctuated by laughs, had been replaced by this calm, like a beatific smile over everything. I kept cool. I suffered fools gladly. Of course there were everyday irritations, the same as ever, but my overall feeling was of tranquillity. No future – nothing I did would have consequences for me, and the past was vanished and beyond help. It was easy to joke about it. (I remember coming offstage to a particularly tumultuous ovation and Norman remarking that they wanted me body and soul. I said, 'Well, they've got my soul – they can have the body in a few months.') Quite funny I thought, but my friends could only react with outraged cries and protests at my lack of taste. If I had made this remark about somebody else it would have been in dubious taste, I admit, but I couldn't stop it entering my head.

I learned to keep these ideas to myself and avoid embarrassing my friends, but sometimes I just had to say it – it was my privilege to be flippant about death. And at such times I really had no fear, I really thought it was funny.

Remember that, apart from the ever-present swelling of my stomach and occasional sickness and blood, I was feeling fit and healthy. But when I got one of my 'false alarm' colds or stomach aches I was less inclined to levity and the audience in my head received my jokes with hollow laughter.

Sometimes I would wish for it all to end. I would shout out loud, 'Come on! come on! Do it to me!'

Somebody had given me a photograph of me and Pete Hawkins in Afghanistan, and I was looking at this when there was a knock on the door. It was Pete Hawkins. I hadn't seen him for several years. He had come to see me having heard of my illness. We talked for a while of old times and this and that. Then he left and we said goodbye, probably for ever.

And there were the dark nights of the soul. Lying in bed at three in the morning, absolutely alone. There is no loneliness like that of the terminally ill – from the moment of my diagnosis I had felt that bubble cutting me off from the world. It was as if I were already dead, watching the world go on all around me. This can be quite a good place to be in, if you want it to be. You can be contemplative, careless, and really not give a damn about anything if you don't want to. ('Taxman! Policeman! You fools! I will soon be forever free from your clutches!')

But in the obscure night there was darkness around me. Just darkness. What did I think then? Not about death as a state, no speculations there. There was, of course, my impending illness – I didn't know when it would begin and what little I knew of it sounded like no fun at all – but right now I really had perfected the method of living in the moment. And in that moment there was no sickness: *Sufficient unto the day is the evil thereof* so I didn't worry.

But when the moment grew dark, it grew dark indeed. Sliding inexorably towards oblivion. All my dreams and memories snapped out, gone beyond recall. It's all so real inside my head, those memories, those landscapes; towering clouds where swimming dragons fly, stupid scenes that don't mean anything at all, stupid jokes that make me laugh after fifty years – millions upon millions of things, trivial and profound, that exist only in my brain. And when that brain stops working they are all gone for ever as if they had never been. Does this matter? Probably not.

Meanwhile, back in the abyss, I am feeling bad. I have a telephone and friends I could call at any time – but what could I say? 'I'm feeling bad, I'm lonely, I'm going to die.' More to the point, what could they say? I just have to endure it alone.

Or watching TV. I remember once being in the grip of despair and the fear of death when something on the television made me laugh. The fear inside me told me there was nothing to laugh about, but this just made me laugh harder – I started laughing so hard there were tears on my cheeks and I was doubled up, clutching my stomach. And all the time the Relentless King of Terrors had me in his grip.

But those nights were long. Sometimes I would try to contemplate oblivion – but it's a futile exercise since it presupposes an observer, which just sets the problem back one step. Or I might let my mind go, 'You, YOU are going to die. Die. Unreal as it may seem, you are soon going to die.' I did not feel fear, or very little, just a kind of helplessness as time ticked by.

I was quite capable of wasting time. I've always been indolent – sit around, watch TV, drink coffee. Sitting on a sofa, watching the shadows move round the room as the afternoon passes. Fully aware that my time ain't long, I sit and do nothing. Wasting time. If I could have all the time I've wasted back again, I'd only be about twenty-five. But I can't help it, I can sit for hours doing nothing. I may be planning some great enterprise to be commenced tomorrow, or this evening, or just as soon as I can rise up from my chair. My heart and mind may be filled with anguish over some task (some simple and worthwhile task) promised to myself. But I just sit there, getting more and more hung up at my failure to act. (All this time surrounded by hundreds of books that are dear to my heart and that I will never open again.)

Hung up about unanswered letters. Worse still are the brown envelopes. I pay my taxes and insurance and council tax and they are always up to date, but I find it almost impossible to open these envelopes – I usually get someone else to do it and read me the contents while I curl up on the floor and moan. My affairs are in order thanks to accountants and lawyers, but the thing is, I'm frightened of their letters as well and I have to get somebody else to open and read them. Oh for those dear departed days when brown envelopes were excitedly welcome and contained big fat royalty cheques.

One significant change in my consciousness was that after ten years, Irene was retreating from my thoughts – I mean I was only thinking of her every hour or so, rather than every waking minute. She used to fill my thoughts all the time and everywhere. I remember in the aftermath of her death being in some barn in the middle of Finland listening to the great Joe Buddy play. This is powerful music and Finland is a mysterious place and Irene's spirit seemed to be calling all around me. In the pines, in the pines. Now she had retreated and taken her place in the fabric of my new universe. But I loved her still.

Why is it that we mourn? Is it the thought of a future that must be spent without the one we have lost? Take away that future and it all becomes one. Irene's dead, but so is the future. There won't be much more time I have to pass without her. It won't be long.

Passing time. One of my favourite expeditions was to the Railway Hotel, Southend on a Sunday afternoon. This, and

I speak without prejudice, is one of the best (no – *the* best) music bars in the country. The interior, and the walls outside, have escaped the frightful kitsch 'improvements' that the beer companies have bestowed on so many pubs. The walls are lined with musical gear – bass drums, guitars, everything there should be. There's a grand piano and a DJ pulpit. In the slack afternoons LPs play – it might be Neil Young, it might be BB King. Lean on the unspoiled bar and have a drink. There are pictures on the walls of heroes old and new. (And, I must admit, there is a portrait of me on the pub sign outside. It's impossible not to feel proud of this, though of course I can't point it out to visitors. I have to get friends to do it – modesty forbids.)

The crowd is friendly. They are there for the music – they are dancing. In the Railway, especially with the incomparable Steve Weston and his band on stage, is a good place to be. Sometimes Steve will feature the brilliant guitarist Paul Garner playing real blues with a feeling (a rare thing these days). It is a pleasure to watch somebody play that thing so much better than I can. Combined with Steve's harmonica and a cool rhythm section of upright bass and drums, this is great music enjoyed in a perfect atmosphere. Please don't change the Railway Hotel.

After my diagnosis became known publicly, it was groovy to walk into the Railway – smiles and greetings all round. It felt good. Then I could just stand among the throng and enjoy the music. Sometimes, maybe after a drink, I would get up and play a number with Geoff Chapman's band. In the sixties Geoff had been a fellow member of The Flowerpots with me, and that gives you a funny feeling, standing on a tiny stage in a

Southend pub, nearly fifty years later. Moments like these make you realise that life is but a joke – quite a good one sometimes.

After all, here I was about to embark on a sell-out tour, intense interest from the international media, TV appearances, interviews, after years in the wilderness playing small venues and lucky to merit an advert in the Yellow Advertiser. Don't get me wrong – I loved the life I had settled into. Nothing to do but be at home and then pack my suitcase and go off and play some gigs with a great band. Lots of laughs, no responsibilities. I can't think of a better way of making a living.

But now I was famous. I had experienced some of this in the seventies and I liked it, so it was fun doing TV, radio and newspaper interviews. At such times, I felt high – like you are when you're doing a live World Service interview with cameras pointing at you – and I would describe the good feelings I had experienced, and how I remained in good spirits by accepting my death as inevitable and living in the moment. I began to receive, or see in the newspapers, letters from cancer sufferers telling me that my words had brought them comfort or inspiration. To think that my words were of help to somebody in desperate need . . .

I didn't preach any method; I didn't give any practical advice; I just spoke about the way I felt. The way it struck me from the beginning. I didn't plan to feel this way (well, who can do that?). My only conscious thought was to accept my death as inevitable. Certain. And no false hopes, miracle cures or thunderbolts would change it.

We did the tour to highly charged emotion from the audiences. It was – I don't know, was it? – the best kicks I've ever had, playing those songs (the Feelgood songs where it all started – all the while thinking what each one meant – the scenes and the women . . . Where are they now?).

I began to receive messages of support from people in the biz I'd never met, like Eric Clapton and Johnny Marr. These messages were a great source of strength to me. It really helped me maintain my stoical attitude to think that there were people out there who were rooting for me. No question of collapsing in a heap and shouting 'Mummy!' Stiff upper lip. The gigs, the songs, the guitar. This was it – this was what I had done with my life. Of course we received a tumultuous ovation at the end, everyone singing 'Bye bye bye; bye bye bye.' It felt great.

I flew down from Glasgow for the last gig in London and found myself suffering from stage fright. I'm not normally subject to this, but after all, I was about to play my last gig ever. I went to the British Library in the afternoon before the show, but all those well-loved exhibits just swam before my eyes, while the rest of me wanted to be sick and run away.

That night at the KoKo in Camden was as good as all the others on that farewell tour. Again the same feeling: to be able to play in that moment – no future and no past. And the only place you can get that feeling pure is at the gates of death. We played good, the audience played good and everybody had a real good time. When I said 'Goodnight and goodbye' I felt sad – this was the last gig I would ever play. And yes, I felt sad.

And I said a second heart-wrenching farewell to Keiko, who had come to see the shows.

*

Then I was retired. I didn't like it. When I could call myself a musician, it used to be great hanging round all day, up at all hours and doing whatever I liked. But when I wasn't a musician it was just an aimless life.

Well, I was still on my feet and cherry-blossom time was coming to Japan, so I kept my promise to Noriko, and Ben and I went once more to the Land of the Rising Sun. I've seen the cherry blossom a couple of times – these evanescent blooms sweep across Japan in a great wave. There are blossom forecasts on the television. The Japanese love these flowers. In the middle of Tokyo people are coming out of offices for lunch and taking photographs of the trees. In the night time, all along Tokyo's winding streams people put down blankets beneath the cherry trees and get lushed out on *sake*. They're all so drunk. No trouble. Everybody happy.

Yuriko said she would come to England to look after me at the end of my life as I was living alone. She left her job and her flat, and got on the plane home with me and Ben.

What to do? I wasted a lot of those days, just passing time. I was melancholy, but still not how I used to be in the old life that I had come to refer to as 'BC' – Before Cancer. Contemplation was often deep, and it was easy to fall into a trance and let thoughts run free. They are gone from me now, those thoughts, but sometimes I can remember thinking after some particularly vivid reverie, 'It's almost worth it. Death. To see what I have seen from here, and felt these infinite feelings.' These thoughts may have been worthless, or they may have had some merit, but one thing

193

I do know – there are deep thoughts and feelings that can only be felt by those about to die.

Other times were less morose – I remember being up on the sea wall on Canvey with Mike and Sherri once for a photo session. It was a sunny day – there was the flat land of Canvey, the water tower at the top of the distant hill, the creek and the path where I had once walked with Irene and the towers of the refinery, the whole scene so familiar since my childhood and I got such a rush of joyful feeling that I threw my arms up and shouted, 'I'm alive! I'm alive!' This intense blast of happiness blew away all thoughts of sickness and death.

The springtime carried on and we realised that the festivals were coming. These were perfect gigs to do – they could be booked at short notice, and if I should fall sick the festival would go ahead just the same. One monkey don't stop no show.

So we played the festivals. Good kicks. My tumour was visible. Growing bigger.

We played at Cornbury Festival, I told the crowd how very glad I was to be standing there, and the people were cheering, and it was very moving and very strange, like a dream from long ago. You couldn't help but play a good gig.

Van Morrison was topping the bill. I hadn't seen Van for quite a while and it was a real pleasure to say hello to him. Later in the sunshine watching Van's set, I felt so very high. I was dying and time was slipping away, but at that moment in the sun, listening to Van doing his thing, man, I was glad to be alive.

Backstage I met a photographer called Charlie Chan. A ubiquitous, vociferous and alarming character, he seemed to be everywhere at once. We talked. I don't know if it was about my illness – but it transpired that Charlie was a cancer doctor.

CHAPTER 22

Along with all the publicity I had been getting, I began to receive awards. I don't think I'd ever received an award before, unless it was for Best Mick Green Impersonator. Anyway it's a good kick – standing up before a big audience and telling them you're gonna die, but that's all right, guys. It's a dream kick doing that. Again it really made me feel happy to see the assembled music biz wishing me well.

Perhaps the strangest of these events was when I was asked to present the 'Genius' award to Sir Elton John at the GQ Awards. I had never met Elton, but I duly took the stage in my Moss Bros suit, made my laudatory speech and then 'Ladies and gentlemen, Sir Elton John.' He came on stage and I presented him with the award. Then he did an extraordinary thing. He went to the microphone and announced that he wanted to give the award to me because he felt I deserved it. And that was what he did. I just stood looking across the applauding crowd, thinking once again, 'Well, these final months have certainly been packed with incident.'

And that tumour was getting big. It has always been my habit to read until I fall asleep and I prefer to lie on my left side. Now the tumour was on that side and when I lay down it would gather into a huge hemisphere there. It was impossible to ignore. If I rolled over to my right side the swelling would flatten and look much less freaky. But I like to read on my left side.

Matthew and Mary came, bringing with them little Dylan, by now a toddler who called me Grandad. We went to the Natural History Museum to see the dinosaurs – me, Simon, Matthew, Mary and Dylan. My family.

Then out of nowhere came Roger Daltrey. Some time 'BC', Roger and I, during a brief encounter, had thought of recording an album together, but it had never come to fruition. Now he was here, saying he would do anything I said.

'We'll have to do it quick.'

And quick was how we arranged to do it.

The record company, Universal, booked eight days in Yellowfish, a small studio in Sussex which Roger knew, and appointed as producer Dave Eringa, a bearded cove much given to bursts of hearty laughter who had made his reputation with The Manic Street Preachers. We also called in Mike Talbot of the Style Council on keyboards, and Canvey Island's genius of the harmonica, Steve Weston.

Now, since this was going to be the last thing I ever did,

and since Roger had said he would do anything I wanted, and since no one can refuse a dying man, I decided to record mostly my own compositions. I'd written some pretty good songs over the years that had been given relatively little exposure, and this could be a kind of retrospective memorial to my glorious self. The title track was to be 'Going Back Home', a song I had written with Mick Green. This seemed particularly apt because The Who, like Dr Feelgood, had been influenced by Johnny Kidd and the Pirates. It all fits.

Putting down the backing tracks was good fun. Dave Eringa proved to be a brilliant producer. Not only was he a master of the technical side of digital recording, but his ear for the music itself was spot on – he always knew when you'd got The Take, or if you needed Just One More, and he could get good sounds from all the instruments. In fact he was turning what I thought was just going to be a good-time bash into a tasty-sounding record.

This choice of material made Roger's task all the harder. Norman, Dylan and I were very familiar with most of these songs from live performances, whereas Roger was coming to most of them for the first time and, without any time to rehearse, had to work out and deliver the lead vocals.

When Roger arrived on about the third day to start work on the vocals he was understandably nervous. He didn't really know any of us personally (I had only met him once or twice) and we, the band and crew, were all getting along famously. On top of feeling like an outsider he had to deliver convincing vocals on a dozen unfamiliar songs. That's hard. Roger is very (too) self-critical and I know that by the second day he desperately wanted to walk away. I found myself in the dream-like situation of having to offer quiet words of encouragement to one of the world's greatest rock singers. But as I said, you can't refuse a dying man, so I had him by the short and curlies, and Roger persevered. He would spend a long time listening to each track, finding his own feel for it. Sometimes he would declare that he couldn't do a certain song, he just couldn't do it, and then he'd come out with a great performance.

One by one, the tracks got done. And while they were getting done, I had concerns of my own. The ten months the doctors had offered me were over and I was entering a strange no-man's-land between life and death; making a record that I might never see released. I would step outside the studio into the night and walk beneath the trees, reasoning thus: 'Wow! this is getting really freaky. I'm really gonna die soon – DIE – but I've had a pretty good and not uneventful life. I've known love and heartbreak and I've been round the world and I've had my kicks, and here I am finishing up making an album with Roger Daltrey and walking here in the dark and the beautiful trees and mighty Orion looking down on me – it's all gonna go and I'm gonna die, I'm really gonna die and I can't complain. I can't complain.' Stuff like that. But those trees did look beautiful and impenetrably mysterious, and didn't Orion look mighty up there in the winter sky.

Inside the control room, Dave was editing some track. Such was his skill with the mixing desk that he could carry out functions without hearing the sound, just looking at the array of coloured monitor screens – and everyone stood or sat behind him watching him do this. It seemed to me that we were on the flight deck of an intergalactic craft, watching Dave pilot us in silence to some remote planet, light years distant, using skills beyond our understanding to carry us, maybe to the Orion Nebula – and all in this cosy, brightly lit control room. And it felt so good, this spaceship ride, that I couldn't help but exclaim, 'Oh man, I wanna do more of this – I'm really sorry that I've got to die.'

As we went on, Roger grew more and more enthusiastic. We had recorded about twelve tracks in eight days and it sounded really good. I think the record company, who had been kept in the dark, got their first listen about then. Everyone was happy. The art department made up a classy black and white cover for the record of pictures of me and Roger in our youth – the company now owned the legendary Chess label and used that for the disc. It all worked out pretty well.

But there were things to be overcome. We were going to do a gig with Roger at the Shepherd's Bush Empire and we had reserved three days of rehearsal time. On the third day, the record company announced that they wanted a video. I arrived that day to find camera crews, lighting crews, and no doubt a gaffer and a best boy all over the place. A person who I took to be the director came up to me and commenced to speak in the most patronising tone: 'Look, what I wanna get is a hundred and twenty-five per cent. You know, get up to what you think is a hundred per cent and then give it twenty-five more.'

I stood there quite irritated by this character. I'm thinking, 'I've been doing my thing for forty years a hundred per cent and I don't need you telling me how to do it better. You obviously don't know who I am. A hundred and twenty-five per cent! You prat!' I remained silent, but I was keenly interested to see what Roger would have to say.

Roger came storming in. He was not in a good mood. He was wound up. He was shouting, 'I don't know what I'm doing here!' Approach with caution. I saw the director walking up to him with his hand raised and I thought, 'Please, please, don't patronisingly pat him on the back.' But his hand was descending. I turned my back and covered my eyes.

'DON'T TOUCH ME! DON'T EVER FUCKING TOUCH ME!'

The musicians were all laughing into their shoes while the film crew looked on at the ruins of their 125 per cent leader. We got on with the video the way we wanted.

Well, the album was a surprise. It was selling. Chris Evans played a single track twice in succession on his morning show. It was selling and selling off the shelves. The record company ran out of copies. *Going Back Home* went into the charts at number three and went on to become one of the biggest selling records of the year. This was hard to give credit to in these last months of my life.

I never had an attitude to the tumour. I didn't personify it or give it a name; I didn't feel invaded by it. I regarded it just as you might regard a bruise on your arm. But it was big and very visible. I suppose I was self-conscious about it when I was on stage, but my guitar covered it, a bit like a seesaw. I could, and did, slap it like a beer belly. It was obvious that it must soon burst, spread its benefits through my body and do me in. What a drag! We're playing really well, doing bigger gigs than ever and selling them out, and we've made a big hit record and any minute now I'm gonna die. Actually, it *is* quite funny.

My ten months had passed, and more. Earlier in the year I had bet French Henri £100 that I wouldn't see Christmas (this is a lose–lose bet), but there I was, and I happily forced his winnings on him against his protests.

Round about New Year we were sitting at home watching a Japanese film when I started rocking back and forth, back and forth in my chair. This carried on and on and Yuriko told me to stop. But I couldn't. I started talking aimlessly, just rapping. Rocking and rapping. It got more deranged – I was yakking like a berserk ventriloquist's dummy, and all the time rocking back and forth. Yuriko told me I was having a panic attack. I said we should go out for a walk. Outside it was dark and rainy – we got as far as the gate and I said, 'Let's go back indoors.' But I was still in a state of terrible nervous tension, rocking and rapping, so we ventured forth again. Along the street in the rain and darkness I could see people walking towards us.

'Are there people up there?'

'No, there's nobody.'

The hallucination persisted, so I just let the people walk. When we turned to walk back there was another crowd coming our way, but I didn't even bother to ask about them.

The next day we called Patrick, the Macmillan cancer nurse. I told him about the panic attack and how I thought it had come on because my ten months was over and this had caused me to panic. He looked at me and said, 'You don't look to me like somebody near the end. I think you've got a good while ahead of you.' He asked me if I suffered from backache and I told him I didn't. He repeated his reassuring words, telling me that he was speaking from long experience.

Ha! Just when I was getting used to it, the end was no longer nigh.

But the tumour was growing and it would not stop.

I did interviews and Q&A sessions with Roger Daltrey, and the album continued to sell. HMV were featuring the record on their TV ads – it's quite a good thing to switch on the telly and hear your name being extolled as if you were a bottle of beer.

Outside Paddington station a taxi driver called to me, 'Where are you going? I'll take you anywhere you want to go for free.'

But my time ain't long and soon I've got to go. The tumour was huge. Soon it must start to kill me.

CHAPTER 23

We had some gigs supporting Status Quo on their fiftieth anniversary tour. I was now three months into extra time and any gig I played could be my last. *Going Back Home* was still number three in the charts, we were having photos taken with Quo and I was joking about not getting any older. I really didn't care any more – I felt that the end was very near. Everything I did, going to the shops, changing my guitar strings, tidying up the house or talking with the neighbours, felt numb, unreal, as if I were an actor in a play. As if death had already come and I was just shuffling around in the aftermath.

But it was exhilarating to walk on stage feeling like that. To play without regard to anything but the show – no future to look forward to, no past to regret. Just the minute itself to live in. As we launched into the first number I felt high, defiant, riding on the groove laid down by Norman and Dylan. I felt so proud of them. My band. The best I'd ever had, and I was grateful to have lived to play these final shows with them.

Back in the dressing room, Nigel Kerr, our agent, was talking of big gigs he was booking in, including an appearance at Glastonbury. I had reservations about this – in all the years I'd been playing on the British scene, and in all the years the Glastonbury Festival had been going, they had never once invited me to play there. It seemed I had to get terminal cancer to be deemed worthy of their attention.

My instincts about Glastonbury Festival proved true when we eventually came to play there in 2015. We stopped at the gate and showed our passes to security. One of them, without a word, opened the back door of the car and started searching through our bags.

'What are you doing? Get out!'

'All vehicles have to be searched before they go in.'

'Not this one. You've got absolutely no right to trespass on this vehicle. Now get out of our way.'

He stood there in his yellow jacket with a look of dumb incomprehension on his face. He was obviously under orders and he wanted to obey them. I was getting angry. Intimidated, he relented and let us through. We had hardly got going when another car screeched up behind us. It was the chief muppet, in an even bigger yellow jacket.

'Right. I'm searching this car.' He actually pulled the back door open and tried to make good his word. I jumped out of the car again and told him to stop. There was a face-to-face exchange of pleasantries while a small, interested crowd gathered. He was telling me that his orders were to let nobody by without searching, and I was telling him that he had no right to assume powers greater than those of the police or customs. If he didn't get out of our way we would turn around and leave, and he could explain to Farmer Giles why we weren't on stage that evening.

The insolence of office! He was adamant that he was contractually entitled to search the car and everything in it. He wasn't going to back down, especially in front of his minions – one of these, a pubescent boy in a tiny yellow jacket, piped up, 'We're only trying to do our job!!'

I looked at him with pity and contempt. We? Our job?

One of the festival staff came up and began timidly to suggest to the security guy that I was rather important to the staging of the festival and should be let through. But the muppet stood there insisting that he would carry out his orders, and that we should submit to him.

Hear you this Triton of the minnows? Mark you his absolute 'shall'?

I said, 'Right, I've had enough of this. We're leaving,' and told Dylan to turn the car round. I was walking away, very angry. Then people were calling to me saying it was OK and we could go through. By now I didn't want to, but the show must go on, so I got back in the car. Really angry, breathing deeply through my nostrils.

The stage manager came up to me when we got in and I told her what had happened.

She said, 'I know – it's terrible, isn't it?'

I said, 'Well, what are you going to do about it?'

She burst into tears and ran away.

The atmosphere backstage was wretched – the food was as bad as a microwave can warm up, and I swear I waited twenty minutes for a cup of lukewarm coffee that tasted like cardboard. You couldn't take two paces without somebody hassling you for a pass. (Your papers! Your papers!) Two of the festival staff approached me. They said they wanted to deal with my complaint, since I had given the stage manager 'an emotional mauling'. They explained how difficult a problem security was, how the vast area of the festival site was a 'state within a state' (got their own Gestapo too), and how it was necessary to do these things to keep order. I listened in disbelief as they expounded this proto-fascism. They were quite unaware of the implications of what they were saying. Did they really believe that I should abandon my civil liberties – liberties that millions had laid down their lives to secure – just for the honour of appearing at this grotesque, overpriced fairground?

Whale-saving Green fascists! I hope they all get eaten by Moby Dick.

A week later we played the Cambridge Folk Festival. We were waved through the gate with a friendly greeting. Two patrolling coppers came up and shook my hand and wished me well; we wandered freely round the backstage area, meeting old friends. The food was good. Everybody had a good time; everybody saw the sun shine.

After the Quo gigs I went home with my tumour and we passed the time. There were interviews and appearances – *Going Back Home* remained in the charts, having become one of the best-selling albums of the year. We played the

Albert Hall supporting The Who. I invited Noriko, who had called me back to Japan to see the cherry blossoms the previous spring, to come to England for a few days. On the last night of her visit she sat up all night with me, smiling and silent while I played my guitar. She found my notebook. On one page I had written '12th of July 2013 – my last birthday'. She wrote *No! No! No!* across the page.

Then Charlie Chan materialised in my living room. He had become curious as to why I was still alive and kicking when I should have been dead, or at least mortally ill. Pancreatic cancer – called 'King Cancer' by the Japanese – is remorseless and swift and spares nobody, yet here I was still on my feet and playing gigs after more than a year. Charlie suspected that my tumour was a rare, slow-growing type of pancreatic cancer. A type that might be amenable to surgery. He examined me and seemed to find confirmation of his theory. He talked of the possibility of surgery, of a cure, or at least of a reprieve, and I listened, shielded in my armour of scepticism as he explained to me the advantages of living over death. It all seemed so unreal. But Charlie was insistent. He said he wanted me to go to Cambridge, to Addenbrooke's Hospital, to consult his old Oxford University friend, Emmanuel Huguet.

CHAPTER 24

Mr Emmanuel Huguet is the perfect image of a surgeon. Tall, lean and bespectacled, his demeanour is serious, almost solemn (but I think he likes a laugh). Mike drove us – me, Simon and Yuriko – to a small clinic in Cambridge to meet him. As we walked in, a couple were leaving. They stopped and asked for my autograph, and the man told me that he had been cured of pancreatic cancer. He was one of the 3 per cent who survive. Could they really do such things here?

Mr Huguet introduced himself and led us into a small room. We sat round a table like students while he explained my case with all the clarity of an experienced teacher, drawing diagrams on a loose-leaf page. He told me that he felt my condition was, in fact, operable and that Charlie Chan had been right in saying that I should have been dead, or seriously ill, by now, so long after a normal pancreatic cancer diagnosis. I certainly should not still be walking about and ·

doing gigs. My tumour *was* an unusual one – something like the one that had killed Steve Jobs. There were more scans to be done to be absolutely sure, but Mr Huguet was ninety-nine per cent certain they could operate.

That one per cent of uncertainty made me cling to my determination to reject false hopes. What if they did more scans and found that an operation wasn't possible after all? At this late stage I wanted no such disappointment. When he began to talk about the various consequences of an operation (I would become diabetic; I would need daily medication for the rest of my life), I said that I wouldn't even think about it until we were sure it could go ahead. But I already knew I would happily place my life in Mr Huguet's hands; his voice, calm and objective, carried within it an authority that inspired trust. I felt like telling him to go ahead anyway, even if the scans weren't favourable. The tumour was so big now it would soon break up and I would descend into pain and sickness and death. An operation could cure me or let me down into the oblivion of anaesthesia, never to wake again. Either way I would escape suffering. Strange shivers of hope ran through me. Yes, I wanted this operation, this kill-or-cure consummation, and here was the man to do it. Mr Huguet became transformed, almost totemic, in my eyes, a being who had come suddenly into my moribund world and was telling me he could save my life. (Is this man telling me he can save my life? Yes he is.)

As we left, Mike and I looked at each other and made the face that says, 'What a guy!'

The scans were done. We went back to Cambridge and Mr Huguet told us that his whole team were convinced that the operation was possible. For the first time in fifteen months I allowed hope, so resolutely banished from my mind, to fill me. I breathed in this strange emotion. Here I was. The universe had changed again. I felt absolutely calm. The future had been switched on like a light.

Mr Huguet stressed that the operation would be a major one. There would be several procedures involved that had never before been performed simultaneously – they would remove the tumour along with my spleen and pancreas and part of my stomach and gut. Specialist transplant surgeons might be called in if major blood vessels needed reconstruction. It could take up to twelve hours. He amused us by saying how, three or four hours into a major operation, when they were ready to start serious cutting, the team would go off for a coffee break, leaving the unconscious patient with the anaesthetist. Well, of course they do – a twelve-hour shift is a long one – but it was hard to imagine these shamans, with their masks and instruments and ritualised gestures, conducting any rite so mundane as a coffee break. He asked if I needed time to consider, not wishing to pressure or persuade me in any way, but of course my mind was made up. When I said I wanted to go ahead, Mr Huguet seemed pleased and said that he would have wanted this had he or a member of his family been in my position. 'Get the thing out.'

There was a day available for the operation at Addenbrooke's Hospital in two weeks' time.

I signed the papers and walked out, shaking my head in bemusement. This year had been so full of twists, turns, coincidences: from a death sentence to international media celebrity, my story in all the newspapers from the *Sun* to the *Guardian* to the front page of the *Sunday Times*; after years without a record deal to have made an album with Roger Daltrey, and that album to have become a huge best-seller; from saying 'Goodnight and goodbye' at my final farewell gig to playing the Albert Hall still alive and well; from awards ceremonies where I would be greeted warmly by a music business that I thought had long forgotten me, to Charlie Chan and Elton John, Tokyo and breakfast TV; to being treated like a star again. None of it expected, all of it seen through the perspective of imminent death. And now this unlooked-for last-minute rescue, too improbable for any soap opera. You had to laugh.

The next couple of weeks were spent in a strange limbo. Was this really the end? Was this crazy final chapter of my life to end on an operating table? Or would I live to look back on it all like a long, intense, powerful dream from which I had awoken in relief and wonder? Was I really going to live? Was I really going to die? *Que sera sera.*

I attended the *Music Week* Awards, where I was to present an award to Roger Daltrey in recognition of his work with his Teenage Cancer Trust. Still in my bubble, standing apart from the unreal world around me, I told people about the operation. 'What, are they going to cure you?' 'Well, they think they can.' (I *knew* Mr Huguet could do it.) Roger said, 'Somebody must have been looking down on you when you refused chemotherapy.' Dave Eringa responded to my news with one of his characteristic guffaws. 'Really?'

'Yeah, really.'

I went to be interviewed by Richard Madeley for BBC

Radio 2. The interview had been arranged to plug the *Going Back Home* album, which was continuing to sell and receive awards around the world. I had been assured that the topic of my illness would be avoided. (I had a slightly superstitious aversion to discussing the operation before the fact.) The interview consisted of question after question about cancer or about my role in the British beat boom of the sixties. I was a schoolboy in the sixties and had played no part in any beat boom, British or otherwise.

The interview was live, so it was impossible to interrupt this flood of embarrassing questions. I had stressed to the BBC that I didn't want to talk about my cancer; the operation was being kept secret and I couldn't answer questions about Herman's Hermits or the Dave Clark Five. Tony Parsons was there waiting to interview me for *GQ* magazine, and having a little laugh, but he picked up on the medical stuff and started asking me about it. So I just let go and told him the whole thing – Charlie Chan, Emmanuel Huguet, Addenbrooke's Hospital, Major Operation and all. In the event it was a relief to talk about it all to someone who was on my side. Not that I was nervous . . .

Julien Temple had been making a film about me during my illness (it would be released in 2015 as *The Ecstasy of Wilko Johnson*) and wanted an interview before I went into Addenbrooke's. The day before going to Cambridge I went down to Canvey Island to find Julien in full *Seventh Seal* mode, sitting on the sea wall with a chessboard and wearing a monk's hooded cloak.

Again he was bringing it all back to Canvey Island in a weird dream. Sitting talking under the westering sun, we looked across the creek to the blue remembered towers of the refinery, my Babylon. The sun on the waves; the big ships gliding by; the path along the sea wall where once I had walked with Irene. Could this really be the end? It had all the ingredients of a finale. Roll credits.

At home that evening we played the movie *Gravity*. These images of a person hopelessly lost in the abyss quite freaked me out, dread of the absolute oblivion of general anaesthetic, my life entrusted to the hands of strangers, gripped me. I was scared. I felt like saying, 'I don't want to watch this – play *The Life of Brian*,' but I grimly watched to the end without a word – that's how macho I am.

The next day to Cambridge where we checked into a hotel, ready to go into the hospital early the following morning.

Blackness.

The little death of deep anaesthesia. Life, consciousness, and the infinity of the soul, all gone into absolute blackness. Nothing. No shining tunnel leading up to the light, no Jesus with welcoming arms, no Buddha's compassionate smile, no demons to torment and pursue. Just that infinite darkness from which we emerge for our moment of life and light, and to which we must surely return.

Absolute blackness.

I awoke in a quiet night-time hospital ward. I was serenely aware that the operation had been successful. I was alive. It was very peaceful. The nurses were chatting, sharing some joke, and I listened to their various regional accents. My mind was quite clear – I had been warned that people coming round from general anaesthetic were often confused as to where they were and what was happening, but I had a complete, clear awareness. I knew who I was, where I was and what had happened. And as I lay there, taking in this quiet ward and thinking about being alive, and listening to their talk, the absolute conviction grew on me that they were planning to kill me. I was gripped by cold fear.

I told myself that this was nonsense. Why would they want to kill me after such a long and expensive operation? These nurses quietly talking and joking about everyday matters could hardly be sinister assassins. But I knew with certainty what was happening. I lay there in fear, wondering what to do. Helpless on that bed, I couldn't call for help – none of my people were there, and all these strangers in the room were part of the conspiracy. Sometimes I felt myself drifting into sleep, thinking 'Oh, let them do it – what does it matter? I was going to die anyway.' Then I would pull myself back to consciousness with a convulsive effort.

I remembered when I was thirteen and had nearly drowned in a tidal current off Canvey Island – that wish to give up my exhausted struggles and slip away under the salty bubbling water, then a last desperate voice within saying, 'No, not me, not me!' as I forced myself once more to the surface. Somebody had rescued me then, but here I was cut off from all help. My friends would surely come to me if they knew, but they were far away in the night and I was in the hands of killers. Remorseless, implacable, pitiless, they were planning to kill me as one might put down an animal, chatting unconcernedly as I lay in an agony of fear. I had to do something before I swooned into a sleep that would surely be my last. I called one of the nurses to me and said,

'Something's wrong. There's something that's not right.'
He told me that everything was good, and that I might be
disorientated after the anaesthetic. Did I know my name?
Did I know where I was? Yes, I knew very clearly who and
where I was, and what had happened. I also knew with
equal certainty that they were planning to murder me. Of
course I could not talk of this to one of the conspirators,
so I said, 'I want to see a doctor.' They told me it was the
middle of the night and no doctors were available.

Of course.

Not to be thwarted, I told them I wanted to see a policeman. I was insistent, and they said they'd see what could
be done. While we were waiting I delicately touched my
stomach with my fingertips. I felt a large zip fastener running down me and hurriedly withdrew my hand.

They came back with two guys dressed in the uniform of
hospital security. More conspirators. I said to them, 'You're
not policemen.' They tried to assure me of their bona fides,
but I knew I was trapped – I couldn't tell these people of
my predicament, couldn't call on them for help. After they
had gone, I lay back exhausted. Still gripped by fear, I was
slipping into unconsciousness. Not me! Not me! I had to
make one last effort to save myself – I knew it was the right
thing to do, not to go gentle into that good night. I stood
up, pulling at the tubes I was connected to. The nurses
rushed up to me, trying to make me lie down. There was
an IV tube in my neck, and I seized the catheter and began
pulling at it. I remember the nurses' hands on my arms
trying to restrain me, but I wrenched the catheter out of
my neck. Blood splashed on to the sheet.

In the morning Simon and Yuriko visited me. The conspirators had been replaced by the day shift, but the fear still remained. I told them I had been through a heavy ordeal but could not speak of it. As they wheeled me out of the recovery ward I held tightly on to Yuriko's hand. *Don't leave me. Don't leave me. Guard me while I sleep.*

I awoke in daylight in another ward to find Dylan and Zoë (writer Zoë Howe, Dylan's wife – they really are a charming couple – paradiddle, scribble, scribble) visiting. Joking about my triumph over the King of Terrors, I showed them my scar – a big Mercedes sign that radiated from my belly button across my stomach, stitched with tiny metal clips. Real Frankenstein stuff. Dylan and Zoë were smiling and telling me I looked good – much better than they had expected. I agreed with them and said I felt fine and ready for a swift recovery. Fortunately there were no mirrors at hand, or I would have seen the shocking sight I really presented. Weak and emaciated, almost skeletal, I would have collapsed had I tried to stand. I was an invalid with a long road ahead of me.

They moved me to the cancer ward, to a private room with a bed and toilet. Outside the window, in the distance, was a sunlit hilltop. With its trees and green banks it looked to me like Eden before the Fall. I lay on the bed, bound down by IV tubes connected to electric pumps which fed saline drips and antibiotics and painkillers into my veins. Despite the morphine I was in considerable pain. My wound was still very tender and my guts hadn't yet started to heal. It took a long time to turn over in bed and I could not sit up unaided. I was helpless.

Mr Huguet came to my bedside every day with his entourage. He explained to me that recovery would be a slow process, that the human body was not designed to cope with an injury like the one that had been inflicted on me – such a wound would normally only be expected on a battlefield. I began to learn the meaning of the word 'patient' – someone who is acted upon, and who can endure without complaint. I had a pile of books, from P.G. Wodehouse to medieval poetry, but I could not, did not, want to reach for them. I watched *Young Frankenstein* repeatedly on my iPad; it made me laugh (a rather painful experience) and chimed well with the big zipper which stitched up my wound. The thing fascinated and repelled me.

Hardly daring to touch the scar, I would look down at my body and see it for what it was – a bag of bones and viscera, a soft machine that had carried my brain around this world for more than sixty years, now ripped open, half-emptied and stitched up like a sack. One day a jolly nurse came in with a little pair of pliers and began removing the staples from my wound. *Click, click, click.* She said, 'I really enjoy doing this.' It didn't hurt, but every snip sent an exquisite shudder through me.

Malcolm, Laura and Yuriko were at my bedside when Mr Huguet came in carrying some papers.

He said he had the reports from the laboratory showing the results of the operation. I felt a moment of apprehension and fear, then he said that it had been a complete success. In that eleven-hour operation they had removed my pancreas, my spleen, part of my digestive tract, a massive tumour weighing three and a quarter kilograms and *every trace of cancer.* They had cured me.

We burst into spontaneous applause, cheering, clapping and waving our arms in delight. Mr Huguet acknowledged our applause with a nod and a slight smile. I don't suppose surgeons are used to receiving ovations for their gigs.

As for me, it had once been my dream to get a place at Cambridge. Now I suppose part of me is there permanently in some jar of formaldehyde.

CHAPTER 25

The first stage of my recovery was to let my digestive tract repair itself. It had been cut to pieces with the removal of part of my stomach and small intestine, and while the loose ends were healing and knitting together no food could pass through. I was being nourished through tubes while my stomach was out of action, and my stomach was giving me pain. I found I could relieve the pain by sitting up for a while, then lying back down on the bed first on one side then on the other, but each movement itself gave me acute pain. My stomach was full of gunge, which had to be removed. Food couldn't pass through me in the normal way, so it had to be siphoned out. This was done by passing a tube up my nose, down my throat and into my stomach. The procedure is not a pleasant one.

Mr Huguet watched as a nurse gently and skilfully did the job. Now, it's OK when the tube is pushed up your nose, so

I kept my cool (just be calm, just keep calm), but man! when it turns the corner and goes down your throat it's no fun at all. They tell you to swallow to get the tube down, but all you want to do is gag and regurgitate. I was in a terrible state – *tears in his eyes, distraction in's aspect*. At the first attempt I coughed the tube out when it touched my throat, and I sat there gasping and groaning and thinking, 'Oh no, not again.' We succeeded on the second attempt, but it was an ordeal. Mr Huguet was encouraging and sympathetic. He told me he had once had it done to himself, just to see what it was like – I call that courage beyond the call of duty.

Once the tube was in place, they attached a big plastic syringe and drew out the contents of my stomach. It looked like cottage cheese – two or three syringes full. But my stomach felt much better, the relief was enormous. From then on the syringe was used two or three times a day, and I had acquired yet another piece of plumbing to go with the IV tubes, along with a drain for some infection on my liver, which emptied into a plastic bag that I carried everywhere with me.

There were various other procedures to fill my supine day. A nurse would come and take my temperature and blood pressure and ask if I had any pain, on a scale of one to ten – it was usually five or six, my wound still being tender and sore, while the mysterious processes going on inside me made it difficult, sometimes excruciating, to turn over or sit up. Then there were daily blood tests and insulin injections for my newly acquired diabetes, and little cups full of pills for I know not what.

The nurses were unfailingly cheerful and I welcomed

their visits, holding out my arm for the blood pressure test in a kind of salute as they came in.

Yuriko had taken a hotel room in Cambridge and came every day to my bedside. I was half stupefied by sickness and painkillers, which made me very poor company – hours would pass in silence – but I looked forward to her arrival each day and, since the hospital allowed her unrestricted visiting time, was reluctant to see her leave at night. Sometimes we would play cards – I don't like playing cards, but it's a way of passing time without speaking or thinking – until the night nurse came in and administered the longed-for sleeping pill.

But, sleeping pill or no, I would often find myself awake in the small hours of the night with no hope of falling asleep. You lie there, trying to be patient. It's no good. You can't be patient when the minutes seem like hours. Too tired to read – among the hundreds of books on my Kindle there wasn't one that interested me. Sometimes there was nagging pain – call the nurse and ask for a painkiller. That helps to pass a few minutes.

But it's still the middle of the night and I can't lie immobilised on this bed any longer. I begin the long process of standing up. Every action has its special pain. It's impossible to sit up unaided, so I roll over to the edge of the bed and get my feet on to the floor, lie there halfway off the bed and think for a while: 'Look at me! Lying here helpless with a face full of blankets contemplating the next Herculean effort in my struggle just to get to my feet!' I felt useless and ridiculous there in that room full of boredom and endless tedious hours.

The distant hilltop outside continued to intrigue me. On a dull day it was unremarkable, but when the sun shone through, it lit up like a little Paradise, a Garden of Eden in the Cambridgeshire fens. Far beyond all the pills and thermometers, tubes and trolleys, the pain and helplessness of my hospital bed, was a magical place where I could be happy and free. True, there was probably a serpent in this Paradise, but that would only make it more fun. ('Hey, man – you wanna score an apple? – Good stuff!')

I wanted to take a photograph of this idyllic vision to remember it in years to come. (Years to come! I had years to come!) The sensible thing to do would have been to ask a photographer – or at least someone with a proper camera – to photograph this distant object, but I decided to do the job myself using my iPad. I would wait for the sun to shine on the hilltop, then struggle across the room and prop the iPad up on the window sill. In practice this meant swinging my legs off the bed, resting for a few seconds then painfully pushing myself to my feet. After another short rest, I would unplug all the machinery from the mains, hang it on my mobile hatstand, and push it across to the window in time to see the sunlight vanish behind clouds. Then there was a painful journey back to my bed.

Mr Huguet and his team assured me that my digestive system would repair itself, but it was taking longer than expected, and the nasogastric tube in my stomach was in regular use. Actually, I quite welcomed these siphonings because of the relief from pain they brought – though bringing your dinner up through your nose is an exquisite experience. After my breakfast I would wait and wait for Yuriko to arrive. Yuriko had worked in Japan as a translator of medical texts, and she enjoyed analysing and observing all the medication and procedures I was undergoing, and bestowing her wisdom on me. I didn't even know where the pancreas was located until mine was gone.

One day, a messenger arrived, bringing me a silver disc for *Going Back Home*, which was continuing to sell and sell. The disc was placed on a shelf, showing the famous chessman logo of the Chess record label. A nurse came in and asked what it was, I said, 'Well, it's a kind of award.' She looked at it a little longer and said, 'Oh, do you play chess?'

What could I reply but, 'Yeah, sort of . . .'

In fact, I never had a guitar with me, or even thought about music, during my time in hospital and my convalescence. I'm a performer more than a musician and I generally pick up my guitar only when I'm about to go on stage. I was certainly in no condition to perform and my musical knowledge has always been really minimal – diminished chords, augmented chords and the staves and dots of musical notation are more obscure to me than Sanskrit.

When I first joined the Blockheads, a notoriously jazzy group, they had to show me things I'd never heard of – a process complicated by Johnny and Mickey's Geordie accents.

'Pleeah an Eeah with an Eeah Beeas.'

'Do you mean an E with an A bass, or an A with an E bass?'

Sometimes, during my early days performing with them,

before I had spent a bit of time studying, I would actually turn my guitar off (a very easy thing to do with an electric guitar) and mime to the difficult bits. In a six-piece band, all you've got to do is keep a determined expression on your face and nobody knows.

As I gained strength, I started to venture further afield. Yuriko would get a wheelchair, unplug all my electrical boxes and fix them on to the chair (they could run for quite a while on batteries) and push me round the hospital, through the long corridors and into the 'food zone'. In the cafeteria I would often meet people who recognised me and have my photo taken with them. It was nice to chat to fellow patients, all with different stories to tell.

We would also encounter Mr Huguet – how he maintained this ubiquity I do not know – he must have been visiting all his patients daily, and I knew from my own experience that he kept up a full correspondence with the families and friends of patients. Yet he still found time to stop and chat. To a bone-idle sluggard like myself this was little short of miraculous. Wow! If I had given even a fraction of this effort to my work I would have had a wall full of golden discs.

Still, a surgeon has to be dedicated and a rock musician has to be a wastrel – it's the way of the world, I tell myself when I want to procrastinate. If you or your family fell sick, what would you want to hear – the doctor's educated tones, or a twelve-bar blues declaring, 'I love you baby but you done me wrong'? But when the doctor's put you right you can celebrate with some rock 'n' roll.

225

I have to say that after my recovery Mr Huguet travelled to Dublin to see us play. He even bought a ticket, knowing nothing of the concept of the freebie – I told him he would always be an honoured guest at any of our shows. Anyway I think he had a good time. (Always the enquiring mind – I saw him deep in conversation with Lofty, our sound man, about loudspeakers and microphones.)

My wheelchair expeditions grew more wide-ranging. Sometimes we went out into the sunshine, to the very perimeter of the hospital grounds, where I could lean on the fence, still tethered by tubes to the wheelchair, and look out across the fields. Once we even drove to my magic hilltop in Yuriko's car – like many things in this life, it was a bit of a disappointment when seen up close.

Eventually we got told off for playing truant like this and had to ask for permission instead of going AWOL.

I was certainly still very ill, weak and in pain, and my brain was very dull. I would wake up in the morning, realise where I was, and that was about it as far as cerebration went until Yuriko arrived and went to find a wheelchair. Getting into the wheelchair was part balancing act, part wrestling match, made more intricate by the intervening tubes, but it helped to pass the time – as did our explorations of the hospital corridors and our forays outside, and my efforts to get to my feet and lean on my favourite fence. Sometimes I would phone Mike up and try to pretend that I was leaning on some rustic fence with a straw in my mouth, enjoying the fine weather. But I wasn't – I was tethered to the wheelchair. Could I vault the fence and run up the hill with a soulful, bounding leap? No – I would fall down and hurt myself as soon as I let go of the fence and probably get dangerously entangled in IV tubes.

This tedious sense of captivity was with me everywhere, whether looking at the ceiling from my bed, trundling along corridors and hospital roads, or pushing my mobile hatstand full of beep-beep machines down to the end of the ward to look at the clock. I grew very adept at telling the time – it involved wriggling and squirming off the bed with many gasps and yelps of pain, unplugging all the machinery and hanging it on my hatstand. (I wonder if there is a proper term for this vertical trolley – to me it will always be my hatstand, and it served me well as both walking stick and beast of burden.) I would push the whole arrangement – sometimes beeping like an airport luggage train – to the end of the corridor, where there would be a couple of night nurses to greet, and the clock on the wall showing within five minutes the time I had estimated. Then I would reverse the process, until I could get back on my bed and resume my contemplation of the ceiling. I did of course possess a wristwatch, somewhere in the depths of my suitcase, but I never attempted to find it. To do so would be to deprive myself of a valuable activity which could kill twenty or thirty of the interminable minutes of the night. Anyway, I always knew the time, almost exactly.

Time – did it stand still? No, it just went very, very slowly. During my year with terminal cancer, *then* time had stood still, as though with the diagnosis my life had been switched off; with no future to travel towards, time just swirled around me in my isolation. And of course I was practising the art of living in the moment, so the passing of time was something I took little care of, except to notice occasionally that *my* time was growing shorter and shorter. Now, I was like someone on an airport walkway, too tired and weak to pick up my luggage and walk, just letting the world pass by – here come the pretentious statements about future economics, each one more infuriating than the last, here the vacuous smile of an ugly painted woman urging the use of some fatuously named body spray – all going by, over and over again.

Patience is a virtue I do not possess to any great degree. I had had more than enough of my room with its ceiling, and its window with its wretched view of Paradise (none of my photos had succeeded in showing anything more than a blurred horizon line instead of that blessed visionary plot) and its slow, slow minutes and hours. Yes, I wanted to go home. I knew that Mr Huguet did not want this, and he explained to me the dangers of secondary infections, and that it would be prudent to remain a while longer in hospital till these dangers were passed. But what did he know? All I wanted was to sleep in my own bed again, surrounded by my books and pictures and stuff. The superb day-to-day care I was receiving? Well, Yuriko was a good cook, and her experience translating medical documents in Tokyo and her love of administering medicine were surely adequate to deal with this final stage of lying in bed waiting to get better. I wanted to go home.

I blush to write it. I cringe. But I actually overruled Mr Huguet and went home. And before you could turn around and say 'Twat!' I was lying trembling, shuddering, violently ill on a sofa at home while a very worried Dylan and Yuriko called an ambulance.

And what was I doing? I was saying (very weakly), 'No, I'm all right – I'll be all right in a minute.' If anybody ever wanted a slap round the head, it was your humble reporter at that moment.

CHAPTER 26

Back to Addenbrooke's (sirens wailing, blue lights flashing – quite a buzz) and back into another room almost opposite the previous one, only with less of a view. (It has to be said that Addenbrooke's, home of medical excellence though it is, features some of the worst excesses of 'modern' architecture to be seen west of the Gulags.)

Anyway, suitably chastened, I was back on my hospital bed. Contrite was what I was. I had an infection in my chest cavity – thank goodness I had no idea how serious it was, or I would have been scared. I could feel liquid sloshing around inside me and every twist and turn on the bed led to excruciating pain. To turn over in bed was agony. There was no position I could lie in but pain would invade it. They put a drain in my chest – it was literally a pipe that went in between my ribs – and a couple of pints of dirty water came pouring out into a bucket I was holding. That bucket became another piece of equipage that accompanied me everywhere and was periodically emptied to make room for more. The fluid that filled my chest was painful. Turn one way and it was painful, turn another way and it was even more painful – it just sloshed around being painful. I mean, what is the point of stuff like that?

Despite my lesson to follow Mr Huguet's advice at all times, I still nurtured a resentment that I should remain in bed with only gentle exercise. The nurse would come in and attach a big balloon full of fluid and it would drip away its hour until it started beeping to signal that it had finished and I had to call the nurse to stop this penetrating electric buzzer – 'Yes, we know you've finished, now SHUT UP!' I just had to lie there while antibiotics and nutriments were poured into me. I knew that was really doing me good but it didn't make it any less tedious.

One source of amusement was being able to ring for the nurse and say, 'Can I have some morphine?' and she would go right away and bring it. You could unplug all the tubes and take a stroll round the room or down the corridor. But it was still boring. Even Yuriko's heroic pushing of the wheelchair up and down corridors, trundling along roads and pavements outside the hospital, sometimes losing control on the downgrades, all of this was ultimately boring, tedious and I wanted to go home. This boredom, ennui, deep-seated spiritual malaise (sulking, to give it its right name) was worrying Mr Huguet and he asked the psychiatrist to pay me a visit. She concluded that I was only reacting badly to a bad situation and needed no medication. I was still feeling pretty fed up.

But then I experienced an epiphany. On one of his daily visits, Mr Huguet explained to me how the people in the laboratory were trying to breed the germs that were attacking me; once they could breed the things, they could find an antibiotic that would kill them, but the task was proving difficult and time-consuming. I suddenly had a vision of teams of dedicated workers looking down microscopes, peering into Petri dishes, working all the hours God sends – people who I would never even get to see, working urgently and with dedication to bring about a cure for me. And these teams included everyone from the consultants to the cleaners, from the nurses to the caterers who brought the interesting menu with a smile.

And what was I doing? Lying there whining, 'Oh, I wanna go home!' From this time forth I would grow up and become a proper patient, worthy of the people with white coats and Petri dishes – they would research like crazy and I would lie there and take everything they threw at me without a word of complaint. (Well, not many words.) I honestly felt ashamed of my wimpishness and resolved to do better.

There were other means of passing the time – Simon bought me a radio-controlled helicopter which smashed into the ceiling on its maiden flight, and a plastic internal combustion-engine kit containing several hundred sub-miniature screws. Hunting them down among the bedclothes provided endless fun.

Probably the main pastime was the wheelchair – the unplugging of the tubes, the contortions involved in getting from the bed on to the chair, then loading up all my machinery, before the complicated manoeuvring to get out of the door. When you're sitting in a wheelchair you naturally adopt the pose of a king on his throne, though actually you're quite helpless. Sometimes I would wonder if I was the king, doing nothing while all this attention was lavished on me. Or was I a helpless nonentity, totally dependent on others, being bundled about and pushed from pillar to post?

I got to know all the paintings, photos and artwork that decorated the corridors, all the signposts to different departments. I even started to get some idea of the geography of the hospital. Normally I have only a sketchy idea of my immediate surroundings – I get lost very easily. I have been profoundly and hopelessly lost in cities, theatres and neighbourhoods all round the world. I get lost if I take more than five steps out of a dressing room. Somebody has to physically lead me to the stage for a show. I could get lost in a phone booth. Anyway, through sheer repetition I learned the layout of the hospital and could tell, with a 50 per cent chance of being right, which way to go.

As spring turned to summer our excursions became more pleasant, under the trees and down the avenues. After breakfast I would impatiently await Yuriko's arrival, sometimes for a wheelchair excursion and sometimes for a bath – it's tricky taking a bath when you've got tubes sprouting all over you, not to mention the self-consciousness of a body reduced to the skeletal, wrinkled state of a famine victim. I really was skinny, with wrinkles on all my joints and my arms and legs like bones. Avoid mirrors! They don't do you any good.

Sometimes they took me out on a trolley for various procedures – X-rays and the like. Once a radiologist remarked
that my heart was performing well and asked if I wanted
to see it. A sudden wave of squeamishness forced me to
decline. Oh, faithful heart! All my life, in sickness and in
health, through rain and shine, you have leapt for me in joy,
you have broken down in sorrow, asleep or awake you kept
to your task – lub-dub, lub-dub – and I could not take one
glimpse at you in your labours. Sorry.

And so the repetitive days went by, each day hoping that
they would come and tell me I could be discharged. I was
practising patience and never asked about it, but I longed
just to lie in my own bed at home. They were very concerned that the secondary infections I had suffered should be
completely cleared up before I was allowed to leave and now
I knew from experience how dangerous these infections can
be. So I had to remain in that room and trundle about in a
wheelchair for a while longer.

Finally the day came. I could go home. I got dressed and
packed. We had to wait for a big bag of medication . . . it didn't
arrive. We waited and waited. The nurses changed shift. It
was growing dark. Eventually a nurse fetched the medication
from the pharmacy and we set off for home. Driving through
the dark. Away from that strange world of helplessness and
dependence and endless days and nights. I was alive – but that
was too much to think about. Really too much.

Arriving home that night, I realised how weak I was.
Walking from the car, I was shaky on my feet, and the
journey from car to front door was exhausting. I flopped

down in bed and looked round the room at my books and paintings and idols from Nepal and Japan. I suppose it felt good, but I was very weak and tired.

And then began the long process of recovery. I had fondly imagined that I would be able to accompany Norman and his band when they played Fuji Rock and Taku Taku that summer, but this was out of the question – I could hardly walk across the room. My body was still emaciated and wrinkled. I used to look up in the air when I was taking a bath to avoid looking at this wasted body which surely wasn't mine.

Yuriko would get breakfast, ordering me like a child to eat it all, then set about the blood tests and insulin injections. I had dozens of boxes of pills; Yuriko had an encyclopedic understanding of their import and she enjoyed filling in charts detailing my progress. Mr Huguet phoned every day, constantly assuring me that my strength would return and reminding me of the severe trauma I had undergone. Although I regarded him as something of an oracle, I found it hard to believe my fragile frame could ever recover anything like its former glory. Yuriko decided on a policy of walking round the block every day for exercise. I didn't like that.

'You go round brock!'

'I don't wanna go round the brock!'

'You go round brock!'

And so round the block we went. Walking slowly, painfully, I would reach the first corner, where I had to lean on the wall in exhaustion. Then to the next corner, where there was a corner shop and I could be rewarded with an ice cream. The remaining journey was an epic of endurance. It's strange to suddenly have your fit body changed into that of a very old man – your brain doesn't quite cotton on and keeps telling you, 'Come on! Quick march!' You try to obey, but all that results is slow, shaky doddering steps. You try and imagine if you could run, or break into a jog, but even your brain can understand that that's not going to happen.

But it was good to be at home. Friends could visit, I could listen to all sorts of music (a lot of John Lee Hooker). Some Sundays the house would get quite full – Mike and Sherri would be there, French Henri, Norman, Dylan, Zoë, Lew Lewis and various other local characters. I would sit there like an old man, listening to their talk; if they went out into the garden I would stay where I was, listening from indoors. Like an old man. (When I told Hugo Williams that I had cancer he said (*Etonian accent*), 'Oh, rotten luck! Still at least you'll escape old age.' Hugo always says just the right thing.)

But here I was, still alive, but weak, frail and on the very event-horizon of old age.

Age – in my early twenties I used to walk out into the fields on the eve of my birthday and command the setting sun to rise up again and not let me grow older. On my fortieth birthday we were onstage just before midnight at a festival in Finland. As midnight came up I counted the band in, 'One, two, three – FORTY!' Then I realised that here in the Arctic Circle the sun would soon be rising again after its dip below the horizon. And now *that* all seems a very long time ago. Because it is a very long time ago.

Mr Huguet in his daily calls continued to reassure me

that my strength would return. He told me that I would suddenly realise that I was walking and moving easily again. But you've got to exercise, and when you're feeling weaker than weak, you just don't want to exercise. Walking up the stairs is hard enough – you don't want to walk around the block, and so things get kind of slow.

There were radio, press and TV interviews. These were slightly embarrassing after all the attention I'd had when I was dying, but I was able to boast like a fisherman about the size of my tumour. Julien Temple carried on filming this unexpected second chapter of *The Ecstasy of Wilko Johnson*. I received a Q award and felt again the good wishes of the music biz, this time – slightly shamefacedly – saying, 'I'm gonna live!' (Somehow it just ain't as dramatic as saying, 'I'm gonna die!') *Going Back Home* had become one of the biggest selling albums of the year and won several 'best of' prizes, as well as a gold disc.

But did this seem like a miracle – to be alive and well after living for fifteen months with the absolute certainty of death? And didn't the chain of circumstance and co-incidence that led me here make it all the more miraculous? I had refused chemotherapy in the first place, and chemo would have destroyed my health. Instead I carried on playing gigs and stumbled into Charlie Chan, and Charlie Chan is a man of great curiosity and energy, and all this led me to Addenbrooke's – I never would have sought their help myself because I was resigned to the death that Southend General had told me was certain. And it would have been certain, simply because they told me it was and I believed them – but a chain of circumstance and coincidence had taken me, without my stir, at the very last minute, to the place where an operation, a miracle in itself, could save my life.

Is somebody looking down on me? No – I could never be so solipsistic. And anyway, there's nobody there.

Meanwhile I was trying to come to terms with my new existence. I was still living in the moment. The future, even a month ahead, was simply not real to me. Irene returned to my thoughts – I was still in love with her and she was still for ever gone. I was still very weak – sometimes I couldn't sit up or stand unaided. I would sit in my chair, look at the trees, try to recall those ecstasies I had felt, some of those feelings that had seemed so deep. Sadness and the melancholy that had always surrounded me 'BC' began to return. Trips out to the Railway Hotel were pleasurable – I still had all the kudos of my brush with death and it was 'Hail fellow, well met' with everyone.

Visit Irene's grave. Her tree's grown big – it's a hazel and grows catkins and nuts, there in that little wood near the sea.

Yes, she's back on my mind, and I'm back in this universe without her, so I'm tied to the old world and its emptiness. Old sorrows afflict me, my sins are unforgiven.

Thinking about her, I find myself in tears – something I never gave way to in all those fifteen months of dying. It's hard to be without her.

> *Went out walking, I recall*
> *Me and my best girl, along the wall,*
> *In the long grass side by side,*

Where the big ships go gliding by, go gliding by.
Skylark singing in the sun.
Something told me, 'She's the one'.
When I looked down into her eyes,
I saw pictures of Paradise, of Paradise, of Paradise.
Every night you look so mean
Staring at your TV screen
Back when we were seventeen
You turned me round Irene, Irene.

Day got colder, time went by.
Dark cloud rising into the sky.
I just sat there, gazing on,
Like a tower of Babylon, of Babylon.
I went wandering far from home,
Left my good girl all on her own,
I went back there, she got the power
See me through my darkest hour, my darkest hour, my
   darkest hour.
Every night you look so mean
Staring at your TV screen,
I got lost inside a dream
You brought me back Irene, Irene.

World keep turning, all things change,
Now you're sleeping in your grave.
Lonely night time, I call your name.
My tears are falling – I ain't ashamed, I ain't ashamed.
All your loving thrill me so,
I can't go with you, I just can't go.

WILKO JOHNSON

There's a thousand highways – you don't live twice.
Only one road to Paradise, to Paradise, to Paradise.
Every night you look so mean
Staring at your TV screen,
Thinking about what might have been
I love you still Irene, Irene.

CHAPTER 27

My strength was returning. I went back yet again to Japan. Standing on the familiar street in Kyoto – how many times had I said a final goodbye to this place? And now here I was again – death did not come, but left me standing here. Again we went to Taku Taku to see the Porollys. Again in that half-empty room they played 'Blueberry Hill'; again it moved me. But this was strange – the last time I had sat here and listened to that song, I was dying, the future a universal blank. Now where was I? Who was I? This new universe was different, changed. Death, like a shadow, had left the building.

Walking in the streets of Kyoto was like a dream where these places had been fading away and were now returning to broad daylight. Just blink your eyes and there it all is, the same as ever, and my time of dying a memory already starting to fade. And I'm a human again, not a doomed being in a bubble of isolation. I walk among crowds of my own kind, no longer isolated, swept along by circumstance to an unknown and, maybe, distant future.

I went to all the familiar places and they were all coming back to life. No longer that feeling of looking on something for the last time – you can't just fake that feeling – you've really got to be dying to experience it. Could I really have been there and felt that way? It was hard to imagine. When I looked in my memory the images were clear enough, but that feeling was gone. Temples and pagodas all draped with cobwebs.

After a few days, I found myself striding along at some-thing like my normal pace. There is an avenue leading into a Shinto shrine that is lined with statues, among them a brass cow which is said to have healing powers. I had been to this cow the last time I was in Kyoto, my stomach swelling with the tumour, and had solemnly rubbed its stomach as one should. Now I was back and the tumour was gone. I don't submit to the fallacy of *post hoc ergo propter hoc*, but I believe in courtesy, so I went and I said thank you to that cow.

And now the tumour is gone, and my fear of death is shown to have been groundless. So was my ordeal a mere illusion, my defiance in the face of death a sham?

The Buddha tells of a man in a darkened room. In the shadows was a coil of rope. The man took this for a cobra set to strike, and his heart was filled with fear, the fear of death. He could not move, he could not help himself, but stood there fascinated by that deadly snake. But he kept his cool. And then into the room there came a friend with a bright lamp, which dispelled the shadows and showed the snake to be just a coil of rope. And straight away the fear of death was gone and he knew it to be an illusion. He had been showing courage in the face of a piece of rope. But in the dark his fear was just as real as if the rope had been a hooded cobra. I still can't work that out – was it real or was it not?

Back in the real world and its uncertain future, it's hard to think about what has happened – I am alive. I survived cancer. I was saved from certain death. Here I am, thinking about it all when I should be dead and gone and not thinking about anything. That fifteen months walking in the Valley of the Shadow of Death is now fading like a dream. It's hard to think about – hard to take in.

One evening in the ancient town of Nara with its monumental Buddhas and pagodas, we climbed the long steps to Todaiji temple. At sunset crowds were gathering – there was to be a ceremony. On the long balcony which fronts the temple the abbot was intoning prayers, and at either end stood a monk holding a long bamboo pole. On the end of these poles were fixed large bundles of twigs. The sun set, and the bundles were set alight, and the monks began running from end to end of the balcony, trailing the flaming bundles beneath them. As the twilight gathered, the running monks were lost in shadow and the two flying bonfires went back and forth across the front of the temple like fiery dragons. And all this time the colours of the sunset were reflecting on the temple. The walls turned red and orange, yellow, gold, green and silver, colour turning to colour in sheets. It was a psychedelic and hypnotic vision, unreal.

243

The fires flew, and the colours tolled their changes, and I began to think – who would believe that I'd be standing here, alive and conscious, witnessing this miracle when I should have been a year in my grave? Standing in a kind of ecstasy. As always, the idea of being alive overwhelmed me. I couldn't take it in. All I could do was stand there and dig it, the colours and the dragons. If only Irene could be with me by my side.

Thanks to my son Simon Johnson for being amanuensis, eye-witness and minder during the writing of this book.